Praise

'If you work in digital, design or technology, want to level up your game in the most critical skill set of all, you'll find what you need here. Trenton expertly distils down all the important soft skills into one concise, practical book. An essential addition to your toolkit.'

— **Andrew Merryweather**, VP User Experience at Elsevier

'Your team's ability to have difficult conversations, build relationships and lead with integrity are some of the leading factors in professional success. I've always admired Trenton's approach to leadership, so I'm super excited he's sharing his secrets in this wonderful book.'

— **Andy Budd**, design founder, board advisor, speaker and coach

'Building high-performing digital teams is one of the most important capabilities for any business and this book offers a very clear framework to help you do that faster and in a repeatable way.'

— **Arif Harbott**, angel investor, technology disruptor, and author of *The HERO Transformation Playbook*

'Trenton helps us understand that you don't have to be a "people person" to improve your people skills and elevate your reputation. He takes a pragmatic, rather than idealistic, approach to communication, teamwork and stakeholder management.'
— **Bede McCarthy**, Head of Product at Channel 4

'The most useful book on people skills since *How to Win Friends and Influence People*. Read it yourself and buy one for everyone on your team.'
— **Jono Hey**, Chief Product Officer at Zen Educate and creator of Sketchplanations

'The genius of this book is it quickly moves from theory to giving practical tips on how to harness the superpower of EQ to transform yourself and your organisation. A must-read for anyone working on the digital transformation of their organisation.'
— **Matthew Phelan**, author of *Freedom To Be Happy* and co-founder at The Happiness Index

'Pretty much everything we do requires us to work well with others. Trenton's book is easy to read and practical, and gives you access to knowledge that can take decades to develop.'
— **Neil Roberts**, Chief Product Officer at Papier

'Packed with actionable insight and challenging convention at every turn, this book will make you want to jump up and start making changes straightaway. Fall over yourself to read it.'
— **Nikki Gatenby**, NED, leadership coach and author of *Superengaged*

'As we enter into a world of more flexibility, choice and, thereby, dilemmas, I have no doubts we all need Human Powered change in our near futures. Thankfully we have Trenton and his book in our corner.'
— **Perry Timms**, founder and Chief Energy Officer at PTHR, and author of *Transformational HR* and *The Energized Workplace*

Human Powered

Supercharge your digital product
teams with emotional intelligence

TRENTON MOSS

R^ethink

First published in Great Britain in 2021
by Rethink Press (www.rethinkpress.com)

© Copyright Trenton Moss

Cover image © Shutterstock | DragonTiger8

Printed and bound in Great Britain by CMP (UK) Limited, Poole

Contents

To Alison, Charlotte and Henry – thanks for being the best family I could ever wish for and for your unending support.

To Mum and Dad – thanks for helping me become the person that I am today.

Introduction:
EQ Is The New IQ

As part of your job, you need to collaborate with everyone in your team and with stakeholders across the business. When teams and requirements change, there's an ever-changing set of people that you need to forge relationships with – both within your team and with other stakeholders.

This book is for digital, product, technology and design leaders and their team members. If you're a chief digital officer, product director, designer, engineer, agile coach, delivery manager or anyone else that's involved in delivering digital products and services, you're in the right place.

You'll of course know that businesses have generally been moving away from working in siloed departments to delivering digital products using cross-functional, agile teams. You're still expected to do your craft (product management, design, development, etc) but also to collaboratively problem-solve, resolve conflict and inspire others. No one is teaching you the people skills you need to succeed in this new environment and there aren't enough genuine role models for you to learn from. This is impacting everyone's ability to make their teams high-performing.

This stuff is really important. According to a joint Harvard-Stanford research study, 85% of job success comes from well-developed people skills.[1]

As head coach at Team Sterka, a training and coaching business that creates high-performing digital product teams, I'm lucky enough to have a job where I see this happening every day. I conceived and set up our People Skills as a Service programme, which transforms people's behaviour and gives them lifelong skills in leadership, emotional intelligence, resilience and a lot more. I've seen first-hand the impact our programmes have on people and teams. Watching everyone develop new, lifelong skills as they progress through the programme is amazing.

Not every employer will put their teams through Team Sterka's People Skills as a Service programme and I genuinely want everyone to have access to the essential skills that we teach. My hope is that you get as much from this book as the people that go through our programmes do.

Why this book is needed

To succeed in your career, emotional quotient (or emotional intelligence, known as EQ) has become the new IQ in terms of importance. Specialist practitioner knowledge once known by the few (and therefore highly valued) is now freely available on the Internet. With businesses working in matrix structures with cross-functional teams, the ability to work well with people from different backgrounds is now the priority.

Most technology projects don't fail due to bad code. For product and digital leaders, one of their main challenges is getting everyone in their teams to play nicely with each other and with other stakeholders. Get this right and quality and velocity of output increases, as well as product and digital teams having a greater influence and a bigger impact on the business.

Forward-thinking leaders create behavioural frameworks and values to try and guide their team's behaviour. Without a sustained effort though (and really, who has the time?) people tend to glance at these and then get on with their day-to-day jobs without understanding the behavioural changes they should be aspiring to. We often don't know what we don't know when it comes to people skills, so we don't think we need to develop these. Most people try to be the best version of themselves at work. If they knew how to perform better, they would.

People skills training can be expensive, plus people often prefer using their training budget to advance their practitioner skills (ie hard skills). Trying to develop your skills in leadership, EQ and resilience can also be hard work and emotionally challenging. Your hard skills will help you get the job in the first place, but your people skills will help you succeed in your role. Remember, they account for 85% of job success. People skills can be trained and they can be learnt. This book will teach you the skills you need to succeed in a cross-functional team and to make it high-performing.

What you'll get from reading this book

With a better understanding of yourself, increased empathy and the tools to inspire those around you, you'll genuinely see a transformation in your working (and personal) life.

Once you start mastering the skills I outline throughout the book, your mindset will start to change. You'll feel increasingly unstoppable and take increasing responsibility for your job and workplace relationships. You'll be able to bring out the best in those around you, inspiring continuously and getting on with people regardless of their behaviour or beliefs. You'll be able to influence, persuade and show leadership to other stakeholders, regardless of where you sit in the hierarchy.

If everyone within your business goes on the same journey, then your business as a whole can be transformed. If you're all able to work well together, leading and inspiring team members and stakeholders across the business, then quality and velocity of team output increases. Off the back of this, happiness and wellbeing improve, which in turn increases staff morale, retention and team stability. This feeds back into quality, and velocity increases to create a virtuous circle.

People will begin to seek help less often, so senior product and digital leaders will get their time back to focus on the things that matter: working on strategy and influencing stakeholders. Our research with 50 digital and product leaders revealed that 70% of team issues are caused by people skills deficiencies.

Get all this right and you'll be working in truly high-performing teams. Leave it out, and you get people fighting each other, zoning out of work and ultimately leaving. Take a moment to imagine it... No more stakeholder politics, no more petty disputes, no more grievances.

What's in this book

The six-part model introduced in this book is based on over fifteen years' experience working with digital and product leaders and teams, interviews with 50 digital and product leaders and a review of more than 50 research studies into workplace effectiveness. I've seen first-hand the key challenges that cross-functional teams face. I've also seen first-hand the impact our People Skills as a Service programmes have on people as they develop new, lifelong skills.

This book teaches you the six key skills you need to succeed in a digital product team:

Conflict resolution: The PLEASE framework gives you all the practical tools you need to resolve conflict. Achieve win-win outcomes that everyone buys into and make stakeholders feel like heroes.

Strong relationships: I walk you through each step of our MASTER framework. Build long-lasting relationships and push aside negative behaviour to create psychological safety for everyone.

Leading and influencing: I introduce a new type of leadership based on empathy. Follow the LEAD framework to inspire and persuade everyone around you, regardless of where you sit in the hierarchy.

Facilitation: Use the READY framework so people emotionally commit to your meetings and workshops. Lead and drive outcomes that everyone buys into and that actually happen.

Storytelling: The DRAMA framework shows you how to create stories for every occasion. You'll tell stories in an engaging way, getting stakeholders to buy into your deliverables and suggestions.

Outbound comms: I give the full lowdown on our RRR-SSS presentation and ABC writing frameworks. Use your comms skills to influence and persuade stakeholders at all levels with ease.

There's a huge amount for you to take in throughout this book, so be sure to take notes as you go along in the form of a self-retro: keep a list of 'What I do well' and 'What I can do better' as you work through each chapter. If you're in a position of leadership, perhaps do one for yourself and another for your team as a whole. Download our handy self-retro template to help you get started, at www.humanpoweredbook.com/resources.

Behaviour transformation takes time (our programmes usually run over the course of a year). In the last chapter I talk about putting your new skills into practice and embedding them into your day-to-day behaviours so they become second nature. Doing the self-retro as you read the book really helps with this.

There's a better way of working together. It will make everyone happier and increase the impact that digital and product has in the business. Read this book and it will be firmly within your grasp.

ONE

PLEASE Shut Up And Listen To Resolve Conflict

Conflict can be a great thing

Think about the most recent disagreement you've had. Picture it in your head. Put yourself back in that place. Remember where you were, who was with you, what the air felt like. What was said to you? What did you say to them? What tone did the conversation take? How did you feel while all this was going on? Chances are, you've got some quite negative memories in your head right now. Experiencing conflict is rarely enjoyable.

Conflict is caused by two or more people disagreeing about something. Sometimes the conflict can last for seconds and everyone moves on without further thought. At other times, the conflict can last for minutes, hours, days, weeks or even years.

We generally think of conflict as being a negative thing, but people often create amazing ideas by disagreeing with the way something is done and then improving on it. The conflict may not have been in the form of an argument, but there was conflict nonetheless. Conflict can be a great thing and we mustn't shy away from it. We all see the world differently (more on this in Chapter 2) so there's always the potential to disagree with each other. There'll be countless times where you disagree with other people (both at work and at home) on a daily basis.

If we harness these differences and embrace them as something positive, then we can solve the toughest challenges and come up with the most innovative solutions. And we can do this with everyone having a smile on their face.

Why we don't like conflict

The problem with conflict is that most people don't have the skills to deal with it. Our fight or flight reaction often kicks in, so people either push hard for their viewpoint or don't voice their opinion at all.

Take Alex, one of the engineers in a product team. His product manager, Charlotte, only talks to him when she wants something. She's always running late, so tells him what she needs really quickly before rushing off. He once tried to voice his opinion but she said she was too busy to listen so he doesn't bother anymore, even though he often disagrees with her suggestions. He's gradually becoming more resentful of her. From Charlotte's perspective, she's pulled from pillar to post by all the stakeholders she needs to manage and is constantly in and out of meetings. When she gets a few minutes to talk to her engineers, she quickly pushes her viewpoint across before racing off to the next meeting. She just needs the work to get done as quickly and efficiently as possible. Some of the engineers don't seem interested in helping her and just sit in silence displaying negative body language.

Alex and Charlotte generally have the same goal: to get the work done quickly, efficiently and to a high standard. If they'd worked out how to manage their first disagreement then they could have built on that to create a positive, collaborative and fruitful working relationship. It went the other way though. Their relationship is gradually deteriorating, and that's lose-lose-lose: Alex loses, Charlotte loses and their organisation loses.

They don't teach this in school

Most of us have been brought up in an environment that's modelled conflict resolution poorly. We've seen parents arguing with each other and struggling to resolve conflict in a collaborative, win-win way. As young kids, we've had parents pushing their opinions onto us with little regard for what we wanted to achieve. Then we grew up into teenagers and got our revenge by pushing our opinions onto our parents. In school, teachers rarely model conflict resolution well. With class sizes of twenty to thirty children, it can often feel like the overriding objective is for them to achieve obedience. Pupils are generally told to be quiet rather than voice disagreements.

Without having the tools to resolve conflict in a good way, things start spiralling. A small disagreement in a meeting can lead to bad feelings between two people, which can lead to larger disagreements over time, arguments, divided teams and ultimately, people leaving the organisation. This all has a negative impact on the business: decision-making is slower, innovation and problem-solving are limited, staff retention levels drop and senior stakeholders spend their time resolving squabbles rather than doing more important things. Negative situations outside of work also affect a person's ability to do their job well. Unresolved arguments at home and breakdowns in personal relationships are, of course, a huge burden on a person's emotional wellbeing. People unintentionally bring their emotional baggage into the office with them, which can contribute to poor comms and lead to further conflict in the office.

At its most serious, an inability to resolve conflict between political leaders can (and frequently has) resulted in war.

Imagine a world in which everyone has the tools to deal with conflict. Close your eyes and really imagine it. Think of all the stakeholder politics, petty disputes and grievances at work. Could we get rid of most, if not all of these? What would your home life be like if you worked together to resolve your differences and came up with win-win outcomes? Imagine if everyone in the entire world knew how to resolve conflict and our political leaders were masters at this. What kind of stories do you think you'd see on the news?

PLEASE framework

The PLEASE framework harnesses the power of conflict to come up with amazing outcomes. I've used it – and seen it used – hundreds of times. At its core is the sentiment that anyone's perspective on reality is 100% valid.

Remember, conflict can be a great thing. It can help us solve the toughest challenges and come up with the most innovative solutions. PLEASE helps you harness the fact that different people have different ideas. It enables you to come up with better solutions than you could have done by yourself.

PLEASE is generally a linear process used to move through a single conversation:

- **P**roblem is explained

- **L**isten and validate the other person's viewpoint

- **E**xplore in depth what success looks like for the other person

- **A**rticulate what success looks like for you

- **S**olve the problem by brainstorming a win-win outcome

- **E**njoy the success and celebrate together

You'll always begin with P and end in E, and generally follow LEAS in that order, although you'll sometimes jump around a bit between L, E, A and S depending on how the conversation goes. You may also end up doing multiple cycles through LEAS to get to the final E, where you get to Enjoy and celebrate what you've achieved. Generally, the tougher the conflict, the more you'll end up looping through the LEAS parts and the bigger the eventual celebration.

The really powerful thing about using PLEASE is that you work together to achieve win-win outcomes. It's not about you forcing your opinion through (you win, they lose) or about you just submitting to what the more dominant person wants (they win, you lose). It's also about avoiding a compromise (you win a bit and lose a bit, as do they). PLEASE is all about working collaboratively as a team with the aim of arriving at the best possible outcome that everyone buys into (you win, and they win).

What happens if you speak too soon?

At the heart of PLEASE is listening first, speaking second. If you try to Articulate your point of view too soon (even if to just quickly respond to a comment), the focus of the conversation can rapidly move away from win-win outcomes and start becoming an 'I'm right, you're wrong' discussion. Your opponent (yes, that's what the other person has now become) will choose either fight or flight and there'll be a loser in either scenario.

If they choose to fight, you might have a disagreement where you both keep trying to get little wins and make sure you end up on the right side of the win-lose split. These kinds of arguments are unproductive and rarely make either of you feel good, regardless of who the 'winner' is. If they choose flight, then they'll likely shut down while you impose your ideas. You may feel like the winner, but they won't buy in to your ideas, nor be motivated to see you succeed. You've won the battle, but for sure you've lost the war.

Whether they choose fight or flight, neither are good for your long-term relationship and over time you'll gradually both develop learnt behaviour. At least one of you will actively avoid the other and, when you do speak, it'll be a tense affair where you immediately fall into the fight or flight pattern (whichever one you've both chosen). If you're in the same team, then other relationships will likely become tense and the toxic atmosphere will often lead to the team being low-performing.

When to use PLEASE

Sometimes an ordinary discussion at a desk can lead to a disagreement. If this happens you should immediately duck into a meeting room. Don't air your dirty washing in public, even if it's just a minor disagreement. Having the conversation in private creates a safe space for both of you as no one else can pass judgement or join in.

If someone else tries to raise an issue over email or team chat, then you should immediately suggest discussing it offline and ask when it's a good time to do so. Never engage in conflict resolution with written messages; without tone of voice or body language, there's a good chance your words will be misinterpreted. PLEASE doesn't work when you're sending written messages as you lose the back-and-forth conversation. No matter how long you've spent crafting a perfect message to tell someone why they're wrong, be brave and initiate a conversation.

You can use email or team chat to schedule in a short meeting if you're unhappy about something. It's often good to do this, as you give the other person time to prepare and don't surprise them with the conversation topic when you meet. Keep your written message short and simple (the longer it is, the more likely it will be misinterpreted). For example: 'I feel like we're not working together as well as we could. Can we get together to chat about this? I'm keen to hear your perspective and for us to work out the best way forward.' If your conflict is with just one person, then book a room or do a video call. Video is generally better than a phone call as facial expressions also help you understand where they're at.

PLEASE can also work well in a group setting. Whether you're involved in the conflict or it's other people in the meeting that are disagreeing, everyone will appreciate you moving the conversation towards focusing on a win-win outcome.

Let's get started with the first stage in PLEASE: Explaining the Problem.

Problem is explained

If there's no Problem, then there's no conflict, so the first thing is to explain what the Problem is. If you're the one raising the issue (the other person might think everything is fine), then don't talk too much about the outcome other than in high-level terms. Simply telling someone that there's a Problem is usually enough as it's obvious that the outcome you'd like is the solution to that Problem. There's no need to patronise or be prescriptive with what you're looking for. The key thing here is to state the Problem as quickly as possible and end with a question to get the other person talking. 'What do you think?' is a brilliant question that can be appended to almost anything you say, so keep this one at the ready in any tense conversation.

How might Alex the engineer or Charlotte the product manager raise their Problem?

Alex might say something like, 'You're clearly super-busy and it feels like you don't have the time to brief us in. The thing is, I sometimes don't agree with what you ask me to do. I think I have some good ideas for how we might make things better but I don't know how to share them with you because you're so busy. What do you think?' If Charlotte feels confident enough to take the issue up with Alex, she might say, 'You take a lot of pride in doing a great job, which I genuinely appreciate. At the same time, I work really hard to meet the needs of our stakeholders and I feel like you're not that interested in doing this. What do you think?'

Notice how both Alex and Charlotte started with empathy. They made it clear how much they valued the other person and where they were coming from. Then, they framed the Problem using 'I' and not 'you'. If you're raising the issue then you're the one experiencing the Problem. Don't start by blaming or accusing the other person – just state how you feel as succinctly as possible and then get the other person talking. Sometimes the other person will be raising the Problem with you. In this case, it's time to start Listening to what they have to say.

Listen and validate the other person's viewpoint

As soon as the Problem has been stated (whether by you or by the other person), be quiet. Just shut up and let the other person speak as much as they like. Your opportunity to speak will come later. You may be thinking, 'How dare they say that? Don't they know I worked all night to help them out and all they do is criticise? They have no idea what they're talking about. Aarrgghh… What they're saying is just plain wrong. They're always so rude and demeaning to me.'

Whatever the other person is saying (and I mean whatever), and however they say it, just let them talk. Remember, simply listening to the other person doesn't mean you agree. For now, control any feelings of anger, distress or resentment (or anything stronger) and just Listen. Do not respond. Do not get defensive. Shut up and Listen. They're 100% valid to feel the way they do and to have that perspective of the situation.

In short, the more you Listen, the more likely you are to get that all-important win-win outcome. Your chance to Articulate your response comes later (and you must always respond if you disagree). You're not trying to 'win' the argument or get them round to your way of thinking, even if it might temporarily feel good. You're aiming to get a win for yourself *and* for the other person. You'll get far more long-term satisfaction by achieving a win-win outcome.

Clearing your mind so you're really listening

Often, you're not truly listening when another person is talking. You're hearing what's being said, processing the words, placing your own interpretation onto the message and then working out your response. Once you've worked out how you'd like to respond, the other person might as well stop talking because you're not listening anymore. You're just waiting for a pause so you can say what you want to say, or you might not be able to wait so you just interrupt (especially if you think what they're saying is incorrect).

If you're listening to someone else and you find yourself disagreeing in your head, please stop doing this immediately. Stop thinking how wrong the other person is. Stop trying to formulate the best possible response, ready for when it's your turn to speak. Instead, start listening with your mind free from thought and encourage them to keep talking. If you generally struggle with this, try taking notes while they're speaking. If your mind is focused on writing down key points, you're less likely to be distracted with judgemental thoughts.

Two things will happen when you allow the other person to keep talking while you Listen free from any kind of judgement.

First, you'll have an increased amount of time and information to put together your response, so when you do respond it'll likely be more compelling and well-rounded. You'll obviously have an increased understanding of what's going on when responding to a two-minute commentary compared to a ten-second comment. If your response takes the bigger picture into account, it's likely to be more compelling than if it's coming from a place of limited understanding.

Second, by allowing the other person to deep-dive into their opinions and having you listen, you're providing space to reflect on what they're thinking. With you supporting by truly listening, you can often get them to see the flaws in their argument without actually saying anything. What they tell you may even prompt you to notice some of the flaws in your own argument.

Showing empathy

When you're in the listening phase, it's essential that you show empathy. This means that you're genuinely trying to feel what the other person is feeling. Regardless of what they're saying – even if they're blaming you, speaking rudely and/or being totally unreasonable – just try and put yourself in their shoes. Why do you think they feel this way? What's going on in their world that you don't know about? What pressure are they feeling from their boss or other senior stakeholders?

Being empathetic is, of course, easier said than done, especially when emotions are high, but with practice you'll honestly be able to do this in any situation. As part of your empathy effort, it's important that you take ownership for your part in the conflict. It's rare for one side to be 100% innocent in a disagreement so it's likely you've done something to contribute to the ill feeling (even if you feel like they started it, you were totally justified in your actions and/or you just wanted to teach them a lesson). Make sure you're seeing things from the other person's perspective here. Simply acknowledging your role in the conflict with a comment like, 'If that's how I came across to you then I'm genuinely sorry. That wasn't my intention,' can work well.

Whatever you do, don't assign blame onto the other person. On the contrary, do what you can to make them feel like a hero. They're trying their best to do well in the job, so acknowledge their good intentions and the things they've achieved. Empathy is perhaps the most important skill you should develop when working in a cross-functional team. It's probably the most important skill you can have in all aspects of your life, which is why I talk about it a lot in this book.

Keeping the other person talking

You can usually tell when someone's waiting for their turn to speak. They get fidgety, they lose eye contact, their body language changes or they try to speak when there's a small pause. This happens all the time – just watch in any of your conversations at work (or at home) and you're likely to notice it. If you're doing this to someone else, they'll typically pick up on this and it will potentially cause them to curtail what they want to say, which is a bad thing. Remember, the more they speak, the more you're both able to evolve your perspectives.

You can actively encourage them to keep talking by grunting when there's a slight pause and saying things like 'go on' and 'tell me more'. Unlike asking a question, this doesn't cause the other person to change their thought process. In fact, if you only say one thing during the L phase, it should be 'go on.' Be sure to get this into your daily lexicon. Nodding is another great way to keep others talking and show you're listening, especially during video calls. Nodding can also serve to calm things down. A joint Hokkaido-Yamagata University research study found that nodding can positively affect how likable and approachable you are by up to 30–40%.[2]

Active listening

Making it clear that you're listening is easily as important as actually doing so. You could be intently listening but if you're not actively taking part in the conversation when doing so, your listening efforts may be in vain. If you make it obvious that you're listening, it will keep the other person talking and allow them to fully explore their thoughts. In fact, it usually makes them feel good and calms them down (if they're feeling anxious or angry), often making them more open to listening to your viewpoint.

To prove that you're listening, that you're being non-judgemental and that you understand, you need to actively listen. Active listening is so simple yet so rarely used. It basically involves you reflecting back what the other person just said to you. That's it. Active listening has an incredible effect on the other person. You'll visibly see them breathe more slowly and start to think through what they're saying.

Your relationships at work and in all areas of your life will improve if you practise active listening. Whether the other person is a peer in your team, more senior to you or more junior you should use active listening any time someone is talking about anything for more than a few seconds. If done well, you'll immediately see a change in the other person's body language and tone of voice. It's astonishingly effective.

How do you use active listening in practice? There are two ways of reflecting back what was said to you: relaying your interpretation of the person's feelings back, and paraphrasing what was said.

Relaying your interpretation of feelings back to the other person can have a big impact and make them feel that you really understand them. You can also relay back what you think the other person is feeling based on tone of voice or body language – they don't need to explicitly say they're angry if they clearly are.

You can say things like:

- 'You sound really annoyed about this.'

- 'Wow, that obviously upset you so much.'

- 'It must have been hard for you to hear that.'

- 'You've been told to do this when we all know you're already maxed out.'

- 'You seem concerned by what's being said.'

The last example is particularly useful if it's obvious from their body language that they don't like what they're hearing. Notice that all these responses use 'you' and not 'I'. This is not your opportunity to pass judgement or give an opinion. Active listening involves putting the other person at the centre of the conversation.

The second way of reflecting back is also really powerful. Using 'you' and not 'I', interpret the words that were said and then paraphrase them. One of the biggest mistakes I see when people first start active listening is to repeat what the other person said word for word. Unfortunately, this can make things worse as the other person can feel patronised and like you're not actually listening (you don't need to truly listen to just repeat a few words back verbatim).

You won't always get your active listening correct (even when you're experienced at doing it). You may misinterpret how the other person is feeling or your paraphrasing might miss the mark. Don't worry, they'll immediately tell you if your comment doesn't sit right and then you'll get a chance to try again. Active listening can feel strange the first time you use it, especially in a work environment. I urge you to jump straight in and give it a go – you'll be genuinely amazed at the results.

Here are four examples of active listening that Alex and Charlotte are using to respond to each other's comments:

Charlotte: 'I need to get this change done today as our senior business stakeholder has said that it's urgent. Can you drop whatever else you've got going on and make this happen?'

Alex's response: 'It sounds like he's putting a lot of pressure on you to get this done.'

Alex: 'I've got loads on today and everything is being labelled as high priority. I'm trying to please everyone so I'll have to work late again, and in the end I probably won't do any of it that well as I just don't have time. Everyone will just think I'm no good at my job.'

Charlotte's response: 'Gosh, I didn't realise you had so many people placing demands on you. That's a really difficult situation for you to be in. You obviously take a lot of pride in doing a great job but you're being put in a position where you don't feel able to.'

Charlotte: 'Are you even listening to me? Whenever I come over, you just seem completely disinterested in helping me and making our team successful.'

Alex's response: 'OK, so you feel like I'm not doing enough to be a valuable team player.'

Alex: 'You're asking me to build some new functionality, but our designer is on holiday. I have no idea how I'm supposed to make a good user experience with this.'

Charlotte's response: 'OK, this is clearly a really difficult situation for you.'

Active listening doesn't work if your tone of voice is patronising or belittling, so each time that Alex and Charlotte respond they'll say it with meaning in their voices and empathy in their hearts. In all of the above examples, Alex and Charlotte may go on to say more in their responses. Ideally, they'll pause after their initial response to see what else the other person has to say. If the other person doesn't say anything then they'll start to Explore.

Explore in depth what success looks like for the other person

Listening and Exploring go hand in hand with the PLEASE framework. When the other person is running out of things to say, going a bit off-topic or getting into detailed solutions, that means it's time to ask questions. Each time your questions are answered, go back into listening and validating mode.

If you've done a good job of listening then you may not need to ask many questions, especially if you've done lots of reflection and validation and provided plenty of space for the other person to keep talking.

Questions you should (and shouldn't) ask

What you ask, how you ask and your tone of voice are really important. While you're not putting forward your opinions (that's next, in the Articulate phase) you must avoid embedding what you really think in a question.

Look at these questions:

- 'You don't actually think that's a good idea, do you?'
- 'Do you seriously want to do that?'
- 'What would possess you to think such a thing?'
- 'Why do you always think it's my fault?'

These are all judgemental and may encourage the other person to get defensive. Asking questions like these is certainly not in line with the win-win ethos of PLEASE. Generally, it's a bad idea to begin your questions with 'why' (encourages the other person to justify themself), turn 'you' statements into questions (can sound accusing), and ask questions with a possible yes/no response (provides an easy way out of being honest). Your turn to speak comes later, so have patience and phrase your questions in a neutral way.

Keep reminding yourself that the other person is valid to feel this way, that they're talking to you from their perspective, that their opinion is limited by the things they know and see and that they probably don't know how to work towards win-win outcomes.

We're doing exploration here and your exploratory questions should be short, open-ended and non-judgemental. Good questioning:

- Typically begins with how, what, when or who
- Doesn't allow a 'yes' or 'no' response
- Includes just one question (ie don't ask two or three questions in one go)
- Isn't leading and your words and tone of voice don't allude to your opinion

Depending on the context, the four bad examples of questions above could all be rephrased to:

- 'How have you gone about validating that idea with customers?'
- 'What do you think is the best way forward here?'
- 'When did our stakeholder say that to you?'
- 'What's happened to make you think this?'

What else you should say

What you say before and after each question is also important. Before each question, be sure to reflect back what you've heard (ie active listening) so they know you've listened and understood. After each question you should follow up with silence for as long as it takes them to respond. Silence provides space and time for reflection and the more of this you provide, the more likely they are to work towards a win-win outcome.

When the silence becomes a bit too long, it's likely the moment you've been waiting for: it's your turn to speak. If you've done a great job of listening, showing that you're listening and asking good exploratory questions, then often the other person will fill the silence by asking for your thoughts. In fact, waiting for them to ask you to speak is a great thing as this puts them in control of the conversation.

Articulate what success looks like for you

Imagine the person you're speaking with has a goldfish bowl for a head and their mouth is the tap that dispenses its water. Every time they speak, the tap opens and more water gradually comes out. Whenever you speak, you pour more water into their bowl and fill it up again. The more they're able to empty their head of water, the more space there is for your water. Try pouring your water in there too soon and it overflows. On the flip side, if you wait for that goldfish bowl to empty, they'll need more water and might ask you to start talking and fill up their bowl again. In short, only start Articulating your viewpoint when the other person has nothing left to say.

When you're in the Listening and Exploring phases, as long as you don't say too much, you can't go too badly wrong. With Articulating, there's more scope for things to go wrong so for newbies this tends to be the trickiest phase of PLEASE. Tread carefully and perhaps practise with someone else before a real conversation.

Always finish with a question

When you finish articulating your thoughts, you can either end with a full stop or a question mark. Choose the latter as it keeps the conversation going. What you've said might not have resonated with the other person and if you don't invite them to respond then you may never find this out. It's important that they're able to voice an opinion as we want a win-win outcome here. You might finish with, 'What do you think?' (which you can use in virtually any situation), or you might use more specific questions like:

- 'You seem a bit concerned?'

- 'How could we go about achieving that?'

- 'What's the best way forward here?'

- 'How reasonable is our senior stakeholder being?'

Never start your opinion with 'but'

The word 'but' has three letters and ends in a 't', just like the word 'not'. If you start your opinions with 'but' you might as well use 'not' (albeit in a grammatically incorrect way). For example, do not stick these phrases in front of anything you want to say:

- 'I hear what you're saying, but...' (you clearly don't like what they're saying)

- 'You've got a point, but...' (you don't really think they've got a point)

- 'They're not bad designs, but...' (you do think they're bad designs)

- 'You're good at your job, but...' (you don't think they're any good at their job)

- 'I don't mean to be a downer, but...' (you're about to be a downer)

If you absolutely have to put a phrase at the front, substitute 'but' with 'and'. For example, 'I hear what you're saying and...' immediately sounds better. Ideally, get rid of the phrase before your opinion and just say what you think. If you find yourself often responding with, 'No, but...' then try switching to, 'Yes, and...'

Don't justify why you're correct

PLEASE is all about achieving a win-win outcome, so steer the conversation away from the 'I'm right, you're wrong' sentiment. You should avoid sentences like:

- 'I asked you really politely.'

- 'I told you yesterday and you agreed.'

- 'I said this was a high priority.'

- 'I explained this to you, and you said you understood.'

Even if you feel this way, the other person may not think that you asked politely, that you both agreed, that it was a high priority or that your meaning was understood. Stop being right and obsessing about being correct. Focusing on the outcome and what success looks like is far more important.

Use I-messaging to state the outcome you want

When it's your turn to talk, you should generally start with 'I' (the opposite of active listening, when you generally start with 'you').

Beginning your sentences with 'you' during the Articulate phase can feel combative and be interpreted as assigning blame (and no one responds well to being blamed). On the other hand, no one can disagree with how you feel. Anyone can argue with a 'fact' because it's unlikely to be one and far more likely to be your opinion. Even if you're pretty sure that you're right and everyone else agrees, it's still just your opinion and the other person is entitled to have a different one.

You should also focus on the big picture outcome and don't get stuck on what the other person is doing wrong. Remember, you don't know everything that's going on in their world and there may be reasons you're unaware of behind them doing something to 'wrong' you. For example, saying, 'You're always late to my meetings,' immediately blames the other person and invites them to be defensive. Changing this to, 'I don't think these meetings are as productive as they could be and I'd like to improve on that,' followed by a question invites an open discussion. 'What do you think?' works in most situations. At this point, the other person might share that they have to meet with a senior stakeholder immediately before your meeting and these always run over, or that they don't think these meetings are a good use of time and that there's a more efficient way of working together.

Other examples include:

- 'You never deliver your work on time,' could be changed to, 'Quite a few deadlines have been missed and I'm feeling the heat from the business, so I'd really like to change this moving forward,' followed by a question. Perhaps they miss their engineering deadlines because the designer always provides their designs too late?

- 'You haven't completed this to a good enough standard,' could be changed to, 'I'm concerned we won't get stakeholder sign-off for this.'

- 'You've designed a bunch of screens that we can't use,' could be changed to, 'Your designs are genuinely amazing. Really, I mean that. I've spoken to the engineer. I'm not sure he can get these live within our timelines.'

And so on. Hopefully you get the idea.

Using I-messaging and being assertive aren't mutually exclusive. Sometimes when people use I-messaging they do so in a slightly tame way and run the risk of their opinions being disregarded. 'I really feel like this isn't the best way forward,' can be said in both a tame or an assertive way (and anything in the middle). If you say this sentence assertively and if you precede it with evidence, data and/or solid rationale, your opinion will likely come across as compelling.

Use your Listen and Explore skills

As in the Listening and Exploring phases, remember to keep showing empathy throughout the Articulate phase. Every time the other person speaks, truly Listen, reflect back what they're saying and ask open questions.

Take a break if need be

If the conversation isn't going well and you're struggling to progress to Solving the problem, take a break.

Maybe for ten minutes, maybe for a day – it depends on just how badly it's going. The downtime will give everyone time and space to calm down and think things through.

When you regroup, you might want to start a new PLEASE process, this time focusing on the conversation you had previously. The Problem in this case is that the conversation didn't go so well, and you'd like to discuss what happened so as to improve your comms with each other. This is a great way to clear the air and get back into your original PLEASE conversation with renewed energy.

Make sure you get the chance to Articulate

Sometimes the other person may not invite you to speak. They've offloaded everything they have to say so might assume they'll get their way. You must not allow this to happen unless you are actually 100% happy with what they're saying. PLEASE is all about getting a win-win outcome and this phase is your opportunity to make sure you also get a successful outcome. If the other person is speaking at length and you're running out of time, you may need to gently cut short the Listening phase so you can Articulate what success looks like for you. Do this infrequently and only if you feel the other person keeps repeating the same point.

Let's go back to Alex the engineer and Charlotte the product manager. Charlotte has come over to Alex to quickly offload some instructions to him. Alex has decided enough is enough and he's determined to start achieving win-win outcomes. He didn't get the chance to state the Problem but that's OK; he's been doing some great Listening and Exploring to help Charlotte empty her goldfish bowl and hopefully make her more receptive to a constructive conversation.

Charlotte: 'OK, great. Thank goodness you're seeing sense for once and agreeing with me this time.'

Alex doesn't agree and he hasn't said he does.

Charlotte: 'I'll leave this with you. Make sure you get this to me tonight, even if you have to work late. It's massively high priority. See you later.'

Alex has plans tonight so doesn't want to work late and given the other things he's got on his to-do list, this doesn't feel 'massively high priority' at all.

Alex: 'Hold on. I'm sorry, I don't actually agree with everything you're saying and I'm not able to work on this today.'

Charlotte: 'Look, I haven't got time for this. I need to go to an important meeting. Please just get it done.'

Alex: 'This is obviously important for you and I don't think what you're suggesting is the best way forward. It sounds like you're busy now. When's best for you to discuss this? I'd like to find a solution that works for both of us.'

Notice in Alex's final comment that he's not telling her she's wrong to talk to him in such a rude way. Instead, he interweaves active listening twice ('this is obviously important for you' and 'it sounds like you're busy now') to defuse the situation. The important thing is that Alex is standing his ground in a non-confrontational way (rather than an 'I'm right, you're wrong' way or in a win-lose way). He's doing so while showing that he understands where Charlotte is coming from and that her feelings are valid. Whenever she's ready to talk, Alex will Articulate what success looks like for him.

Solve the problem by brainstorming a win-win outcome

Einstein is popularly misattributed as saying that if he had an hour to solve a problem, he'd spend fifty-five minutes thinking about the problem and five minutes thinking about solutions. This approach applies to PLEASE: once you get to the S phase, it's usually plain sailing (especially as you've made it through the tricky Articulate phase).

Don't go all out to persuade the other person. Don't impose your solutions. Just state the outcome you want and be quiet. Re-use the techniques from the Listen, Explore and Articulate parts of PLEASE and you'll be amazed at how easily you can coach other people to come up with great solutions to reach that outcome. Sometimes you'll need to use persuasion techniques (you'll hear all about these in Chapter 3).

If someone offers a solution that you don't think will work, then don't say so. If you do, you're making them wrong (and making yourself right). Instead, reflect back what has been said and ask open-ended questions to help the other person work out the feasibility of the idea (ie all your Listen and Explore techniques). You'll be amazed at how often people go on to circumvent reasons why an idea won't work and come up with something really brilliant.

If you also have ideas then you should share these. Don't do a hard sell though and avoid superlatives and grand statements about why your ideas are the best thing since sliced bread. After you've succinctly shared your ideas, you'll of course follow up with, 'What do you think?' to encourage an open discussion. Remember, you have no interest in being correct. Instead, your sole focus is to collectively come up with the best possible outcome. By problem-solving this way, everyone buys into the solution, making it more likely to happen. When you create a safe environment, you'll be pleasantly surprised at how good some of the solutions are (and often better than the solutions you'd come up with in your head beforehand).

You might also want to do a quick PLEASE after you've Solved the problem, particularly if you feel the other person didn't speak to you in a constructive way (only do this if there's no one else present). If they brought the original problem to you and were stressed, then once you've solved it you might say, 'I'm genuinely pleased we could come to an agreement here. I've got to say, I didn't really like the way you were talking to me at the start of the conversation. I felt a bit like I was being blamed and told off. What do you think?'

You've hopefully reached a good outcome from the main PLEASE process so it's likely that they'll be receptive to your problem statement and you'll move through the new PLEASE process in less than a minute. (If they're not receptive, keep reading. I'll talk more about responding to negative behaviour in the next chapter.)

Enjoy the success and celebrate together

The best part of the PLEASE framework is finishing it. Stop for a moment to acknowledge the work that you've all done. If the process was smooth then this might just be a quick acknowledgement at the end of a meeting about how you worked well together to reach a great outcome. As usual, append whatever you say with, 'What do you think?' to check everyone else agrees. If the PLEASE process has been particularly arduous and taken a long time (which it can do for big business decisions) then you should get together specifically to celebrate what you've all achieved.

Acknowledging success is important as it creates and maintains an upward spiral in your relationships with the people you work with. If you all feel good about what you've achieved together then you'll all go into the next PLEASE process feeling positive, making it more likely that you'll get a good outcome again.

Finally, don't use the Enjoy phase to seek a moral victory and sneak in an 'I'm right, you're wrong' statement (you'll undo all your good work if you do). 'See, that wasn't so hard', 'I told you so' and 'I'm glad you came around to my way of thinking' statements almost always wind people up. Instead, focus on the road ahead even if the other person hasn't given you the apology you were looking for. Just because someone doesn't acknowledge something, it doesn't mean they don't get it.

In summary

There you have it, your end-to-end process for resolving conflict:

- **P**roblem is explained
- **L**isten and validate the other person's viewpoint
- **E**xplore in depth what success looks like for the other person
- **A**rticulate what success looks like for you
- **S**olve the problem by brainstorming a win-win outcome
- **E**njoy the success and celebrate together

PLEASE is a linear process. Go through the six stages any time you disagree with someone or they disagree with you.

As with anything, practice makes perfect. When you're at work tomorrow, give PLEASE a go the moment you spot a disagreement. Remember, most disagreements are minor so they're not always easy to notice. In particular, focus on doing these things:

☐ Don't make the other person wrong. Their opinion is valid no matter how strongly you disagree.

☐ Actively listen so they can empty out all their thoughts (drain that goldfish bowl). Only then should you think about responding.

☐ Take a stand for reaching a win-win outcome. It's not OK for you to lose and it's also not OK for the other person to lose.

Grab a handy copy of these and a summary of the other best practices in this book at www.humanpowered-book.com/resources. Get going with your self-retro if you haven't started it already. Write up a list of 'What I do well' and 'What I can do better' against all the key points in this chapter, perhaps starting with the three focus points I've just listed.

Once you get your head around the PLEASE process, you'll end up using it (or elements of it) multiple times every day. The skills in this chapter are the foundational people skills that underpin everything else you'll read in this book.

Now you know all about resolving conflict, your relationships will hopefully be more productive and you'll experience an increased number of win-win outcomes. In the next chapter, we'll look at how you can build on this to become a MASTER of strong relationships.

TWO

Become A Relationship MASTER

Relationships are everything

We all used to sit comfortably in our siloed departments, sticking with our kind and making whispers
about the other teams and their strange ways of working. We interacted with them a bit, but mostly it was
the department heads and directors that would breach
the demilitarised zone to interact with their peers from
the other teams.

Oh, how times have changed.

Most organisations now operate a matrix structure.
You're notionally in a team with people of your type,
but you work in a cross-functional team alongside
people with different personality types, different

needs and different communication styles on a daily basis. You've also got stakeholders across the business that you need to gather requirements from and then inspire and influence to assure them that the work you're doing is right for them, the business and your customers.

In the modern world of matrix structures, relationships are everything. Building rapport and developing mutually beneficial relationships are key to success in any role, and none more so than when working in a cross-functional team. You might like spending time with people doing the same role as you and who you can easily relate to, but you have to spend most of your time with people from different backgrounds.

Negative behaviour

If you want to have strong, long-lasting relationships with people then negative behaviour simply can't be present. Negative behaviour is any kind of behaviour that reduces another person's wellbeing or growth as a person. It runs on a scale from mild to severe. At its most mild it can be a bit irritating; at its most severe you'll likely feel that you're being bullied.

Everyone exhibits negative behaviour from time to time (although a small minority do it frequently). We don't usually realise we're doing it; we're being triggered and are subconsciously reacting to the other person. On the occasions we do know we're doing it, it's often to protect ourselves as we believe the other person is exhibiting negative behaviour towards us.

Even if you've devoured Chapter 1 and have the PLEASE framework tattooed onto your brain (metaphorically of course), you can still exhibit negative behaviour. We're all human, after all. Negative behaviours can broadly be grouped into three categories: making other people wrong, making yourself correct and gaining power.

Making other people wrong

This is probably the most common negative behaviour category and can show up in many different ways:

- Stonewalling other people by evading them and being generally disengaged.

- Belittling people's opinions or being disinterested in what they have to say.

- Blaming other people for things that you think have gone wrong.

- Criticising others (either proactively for what you see them doing or reactively for what they've done).

- Being rude, grumpy and/or sarcastic.

We all have different personality types, different ways of working, different opinions, different strengths and different weaknesses. Something that comes naturally to you may not to someone else or something that you view as being important may not be to someone else. This can be frustrating and cause you to think less of them or make you feel they're no good at their job. Once you start to feel this way, it can be hard for you to think favourably of that person again. Even if you don't overtly say it, your body language and tone of voice make it clear that you think they're wrong.

Making yourself correct

As well as making other people wrong, we often strive to make ourselves correct. Some of the main ways we do this include:

- Talking profusely so people give up trying to offer their opinion.

- Being defensive and generally engaging in self-protectionism.

- Justifying our opinions with 'facts' and strong statements.

- Playing one-upmanship and always having an answer (ie whatever they say, you know more or have done better).

- Telling people that you were right all along (eg 'I told you so').

You may have a definitive answer about the best way forward but someone else might think differently. You can either engage with them constructively to try to reach consensus and a win-win outcome or you can push for win-at-all-costs, making sure that you're right and pushing your agenda through. You may win some of the time, but you'll struggle to get people buying into your suggestions or willing to go on the journey with you. You'll win the battle, but you may well lose the war.

Gaining power

Perhaps the worst of the three categories, gaining power can be the most challenging to deal with as it's often the least rational. Some examples of when we do this include:

- Regularly being late for other people's meetings (and expecting everyone to be on time for your meetings).

- Often reacting in an angry manner so people become afraid of you.

- Interrupting people in conversation, usually to change the topic (sometimes with innocent-sounding questions).

- Being visibly distracted in other people's meetings (eg checking emails but then expecting others to pay attention at your meetings).

- Quickly shutting down people's suggestions, either with words or just silence.

Gaining power can make you feel good in the short-term, but long-term there's often no real benefit. As with all negative behaviour, you can cause great damage to your relationships with people on the receiving end and with other people that witness your behaviour.

MASTER framework

By now, you'll hopefully be PLEASEing everyone you work with, resolving conflict and achieving win-win outcomes left, right and centre. You'll also be trying your best to avoid exhibiting negative behaviours, but how can you reduce the amount of discord that you have in the first place? How do you set yourself up so that everyone around you is ready to support you in achieving your goals? You need to become a MASTER of building relationships:

- **M**ap out people's communication styles
- **A**djust your communication style accordingly
- **S**uppress your negative behaviour
- **T**ake ownership of difficult situations
- **E**mpathise and assume the best of intentions
- **R**eframe for strength and resilience

Unlike PLEASE, MASTER isn't a linear process; it's more of a timeline. You'll do M and A when you meet new people; S and T is how you relate to someone when they're exhibiting negative behaviour and then E and R is how you deal with the aftermath of difficult situations.

Map out people's communication styles

To build up strong relationships, you need to first work out how people like to communicate. Fortunately, humans are remarkably similar so there's not as much to this as you might think. There are many personality profiling methods, but when it comes to building up strong relationships it's all about communication. Mapping out people's communication styles means you can Adjust how you communicate with them. According to Tony Alessandra's book *The Platinum Rule: Discover the four basic business personalities and how they can lead you to success*, people generally sit somewhere between being Guarded vs Open and somewhere between being Indirect vs Direct.[3] Once you work out roughly where people are, you can approach your communications in a tailored way.

Axis 1: Guarded vs open

When faced with a task that needs completing, there are two different approaches. People that are guarded tend to be task-oriented. They base their thinking on logic and facts. There's no place for emotions. It's all about coming up with the best possible outcome. They love to tackle problems and come up with solutions and will dive in before thinking about any ramifications for people or considering people's feelings. Guarded people can still be caring, kind and empathetic, but their initial focus is working out the best way of getting to a good solution. Only then will they consider the people that might need to be involved and retrofit them into appropriate roles to help with solving the problem. If there's no place for someone, or someone else's nose is out of joint? Sorry, individual needs aren't as important as reaching the optimal solution.

On the other hand, people that are open are primarily interested in relationship building. They'll always focus on people and relationships first when completing a task. They'll engage all the stakeholders that might need to be involved in decision-making and get everyone onboard. Only then will they (collaboratively, of course) set about completing the task. People that are open tend to rely more on their intuition, emotions and group consensus. While their solutions tend to be less grounded in logic, they can be more creative and think outside the box more compared to guarded people.

In reality, few people are fully guarded or fully open – we all sit somewhere on the spectrum between the two. Where do you think you sit? How much of each profile resonates with you? What about your colleagues?

Axis 2: Indirect vs direct

There are also two different approaches when it comes to how strongly you put across your opinions. People falling into the indirect category tend to be methodical, cautious, slow-moving and detail-oriented. They'll listen more than they talk and it can take time for them to put across their points of view. They're also risk-averse so may be reluctant to commit to deadlines and / or specific deliverables. They'll usually ask, 'How do we get there?' and listen intently to the answer, dissecting it to the finest detail.

On the other hand, people that are direct are far more likely to put their point of view across quickly. You won't need to ask what they think – they'll tell you unprompted. A common question that direct people ask is, 'Where are we going?' They're at their happiest envisioning a brighter future and you won't find them slowing down to plan things out in detail. They think fast and act fast and are comfortable making decisions and taking risks.

Again, we all sit somewhere along the axis of how direct we are. Which of the two extremes resonate the most with you? How indirect or direct are your colleagues?

Adjust your communication style accordingly

Dr Alessandra identifies four communication styles in his book and in reality, we all exhibit a bit of each: Director, Thinker, Socialiser and Relator. Some of us are dominant in just one style; other people are primarily a blend of two styles and a few people sit in the middle and are a mix of all four.

We tend to communicate in a way that works for our own communication style and it can feel anathema to do otherwise. You should be Adjusting your communications to work well with each style, wherever people sit along the axes. This can be especially tricky for people that are the opposite to you. If you communicate in a way that best resonates with your audience, you'll instantly build rapport, increase your influence and form stronger relationships. People will feel like you understand them and their needs and that your ways of thinking are aligned.

Let's take a look at Alessandra's four communication styles and my advice on how to adjust the way you communicate accordingly:

1. Directors (guarded, direct)

2. Thinkers (guarded, indirect)

3. Socialisers (open, direct)

4. Relators (open, indirect)

Directors (guarded, direct)

Directors get the most amount of joy out of setting goals and even more joy achieving them. Find out what their goals are and then make it crystal clear that you're supporting them with achieving these. Forget about personal chat or small talk – they'll only be interested in getting to know you (or you getting to know them) once they're on their way to achieving their goals. Directors are at their best accepting big picture challenges and then being left alone to work out how to get there. Make it clear you're there to support them if they decide that they need you and then leave them alone. Whatever you do, don't get bogged down in the details. You might be fascinated by all the ins and outs of what you've been working on, but it's unlikely that they'll be. Explain succinctly how your solutions will help achieve the stipulated goals, and then ask if they want to know more (they probably won't).

They also like to be in charge, so let them take control of meetings and drive the agenda. If there are things you'd like to discuss, then share these in advance so they can work out in which order they'd like to talk through it all. Don't force a power struggle to garner respect. They won't like it, and they won't like you.

Directors are often fast talkers and fast thinkers. They generally like to talk while they think and make decisions in the moment. If you have ideas then throw these into the mix, but let them work out the best way forward. You'll need to accept that a quick decision without all the facts is likely to be made, so think fast and get your opinions across quickly.

In summary, with Directors, be super-efficient and competent. Forget personal chat and just get on with demonstrating how you'll help them accomplish their goals.

Thinkers (guarded, indirect)

Thinkers are often in delivery roles – you'll find a lot of engineers in this group. They're methodical types, so be careful about interrupting them when they look busy. Be respectful and request time with them rather than just initiating a conversation on the fly.

Go out of your way to understand their thought processes, how they made certain decisions and the intricacies of how they've solved problems along the way. Thinkers love talking about this. Make it clear that they're very competent for having done what-ever it is that they've done, and that you wouldn't have been able to do that. Don't play one-upmanship and make out like you're more intelligent. Don't rush them either. Busy product managers (like Charlotte in Chapter 1) may feel they don't have time to get into the details, but this is what engineers like Alex (who works with Charlotte) need. They're not generally into small talk so Charlotte can just crack on with talking about work.

If you want Thinkers to move faster and / or think bigger picture, make this clear and then give them time to work out how they're going to do this. They love problem-solving after all. Don't push them into a hurried answer in the heat of the moment – you probably won't get one. (Even if you do, there's a possibility they'll just tell you what you want to hear to get you off their backs and then work out a way of not doing it later.)

In summary, with Thinkers, be thorough, well-prepared and patient. Don't bother with small talk and let them ask questions and explore as much detail as they'd like to.

Socialisers (open, direct)

Socialisers are the dreamers in your organisation. They're the creative leaders that don't think in a structured way. They tend to be brilliant at what they do but can be a challenge to work with due to their lack of structure. Storytelling is your best friend when communicating with Socialisers (more on this in Chapter 5). Don't explain your best ideas or talk through your work in a structured, linear fashion. Instead, show beautiful outputs and tell stories of how you got there. Inspire them by sharing the emotional journey you've been on. Never use boring-looking slides with reams of text (more on slides in Chapter 6) and don't spend too long backing up your arguments with data or your words may slide off them like water off a duck's back.

Do a good job of storytelling and they'll likely get excited, building on your ideas with some of their own. Their ideas might sometimes sound far-fetched, but withhold your apprehension for now. Share their excitement and join them in dreaming about a better future. They're thinking aloud and might not action these ideas anyway, so let them enjoy the limelight.

Above all, savour your time with them as they want you to enjoy their company. Socialisers are sensitive and intuitive people that pick up on the slightest body language or facial expression cues, so be careful to exude enjoyment. At the end of any meeting, be sure to write up the actions, as they're unlikely to.

In summary, with Socialisers, be interested in them and complimentary. Make it obvious that you're enjoying your time together and don't worry about sticking rigidly to the agenda.

Relators (open, indirect)

Of the four groups, Relators are the most focused on everyone else's wellbeing. You'll primarily find them in roles which have plenty of person-to-person inter-actions and involve lots of teamwork. When you meet with them, talk about feelings (yours and theirs), no matter how strange it might feel. You'll build a stronger connection by opening up and showing some vulnerability.

Take the time to connect with them as people and resist the temptation to jump straight into problem-solving. Relators are at their best when working with people they trust, and building trust takes time. When they speak, be attentive to what they say, slow the pace down and calmly take in their words. Ask questions and show genuine interest in them. In short, you'll be using your new listening and empathy skills that you've learnt from PLEASE.

Relators need gentle encouragement to get started with solving problems. Whatever you do, don't only use facts and figures to drive your point home – it just won't work. Instead, also have everyone's needs and opinions to hand, as that's what's ultimately going to drive decision-making.

Allow plenty of time for face-to-face discussion and potentially extra time for additional thinking and for Relators to consult with other stakeholders. Keep checking in that you're on the same page. There's nothing a Relator dislikes much more than a misunderstanding. Decisions aren't going to be made quickly, but when they are it's likely that everyone will buy into them.

In summary, with Relators, be non-threatening and truly sincere. Really get to know them and give them time and space to progress things.

Find out your style

Take my short quiz and find out your primary communication style at www.humanpoweredbook.com/comms-quiz. Note your position on the graph – the closer to the centre, the more blended you are. And the further you are towards a corner, the more dominant you are in that communication style.

Suppress your negative behaviour

Out of those four communication styles, which resonated the most with you? Which one has behaviour that tends to annoy and frustrate you the most? It's likely the opposite to yours. There's no right or wrong when it comes to communication styles. Every organisation needs a mix of people across all the different styles as each has its own strengths and weaknesses.

If someone has a different communication style then it can easily trigger a negative reaction in you. Most people won't think to adjust their communication style to what works best for you. (As a starting point, lend them this book once you've finished it.)

To develop strong relationships with everyone you work with, you need to Adjust your communications to suit them and then fully accept how they do things. You mustn't get upset or angry by their action or inaction. A one-size-fits-all approach simply doesn't work when it comes to communicating.

Take Henry, a product director. He'd love to get the designers in his product teams presenting their ideas to other stakeholders, but every time they do, they get so bogged down in the detail that it ends up embarrassing him. Now he gets them to brief him on their work so he can do the presentations himself, but it's taking up so much of his time that he's starting to feel resentful towards them. He tried telling them to present more of a 'bigger picture' but it seemed to fall on deaf ears. Or what about Alison, a design director. She's full of great ideas for how to improve the product, but every time she talks to the engineers, they seem disengaged. She feels they only think about delivering the next widget and aren't interested in any of the opportunities they have to delight customers and it's really starting to upset her.

If you don't do this...

Thinking big picture comes naturally to Henry (his dominant communication style is Director), so he simply can't understand how the designers aren't able to do so (they lean more towards being Relators and Thinkers). He's failing to recognise that their detail-oriented approach (which he doesn't have and so doesn't appreciate) is what enables them to create designs that work really well for users. Alison (a strong Socialiser) doesn't get the engineers' reaction to her great ideas. She's thinking up game-changing ways of doing things. How can they possibly not get excited? The thing is, engineers often aren't into blue-sky thinking (their dominant style leans towards Thinker). They methodically and diligently create complex code to power even more complex technical products. Alison doesn't have an appreciation for this because it's just not how she's wired.

Both Henry and Alison are being triggered. They're getting increasingly frustrated by other people's communication styles. They're judging the designers and engineers by their own standards and values and by the things that are important to them. In both these instances, the designers and engineers will pick up on Henry and Alison's frustrations and their respective relationships will likely deteriorate over time. When relationships between teams and leaders break down, team morale plummets and quality and velocity of output are reduced.

See it, say it, stop it

Henry and Alison need to do two things here.

First, they should read Chapter 1 and learn to use the PLEASE framework. They can state the Problem to the designers and engineers respectively, and then Listen to and Explore their perspectives. Henry and Alison would then Articulate what success looks like for them, before Solving the problem with the designers and engineers by brainstorming a win-win outcome.

Second, they need to be aware of their triggers. If Henry and Alison don't do this, their frustrations can boil over into negative behaviour towards the designers and engineers.

To find out if you've been exhibiting negative behaviour, you need to get feedback from people you work with. Show the list of negative behaviours at the start of this chapter to a few people you trust and ask them:

- Which negative behaviours do you think I display?

- What have you witnessed me do with you and/or others?

- What's the impact been on our relationship (or on my relationship with other people)?

You may be surprised at some of the answers.

Now make a decision as to whether you want to rein in your negative behaviour (hopefully you do) and ask these same people to hold you to account on this. According to the American Society of Training and Development, you're 10% likely to complete a goal if you only think about it, rising to 65% if you commit to someone else that you'll do it.[4]

Once you've made the commitment to change, simply follow the 'See it, say it, stop it' process any time the behaviour arises:

- 'See it' is when you notice the negative behaviour occurring.

- 'Say it' is the tricky part. This is when you pause the meeting to tell the others what's happened, ideally apologise and then explain you're working on improving some of your behaviours. The first time you do this might feel a bit strange. The people you're with will likely appreciate it though, as you'll be restoring psychological safety to the room. For example, if you find yourself interrupting people a lot, you might say: 'Hold on, I just interrupted you there and changed the topic. I'm sorry about that; I do it quite a lot and I'm trying to stop. Do you mind if we go back to what you were saying?'

- 'Stop it' is as easy as 'See it'. Just don't behave that way again in the current conversation. Once you've done 'Say it' and made a public commitment to stopping your behaviour, it's remarkably easy to stop.

Finally, celebrate your behaviour. Everyone exhibits negative behaviour, but few people are brave enough to do something about it. So, genuinely well done.

Take ownership of difficult situations

Identifying your triggers and Suppressing your negative behaviour will help you build up strong relationships, but negative behaviour runs both ways. By taking ownership of difficult situations, you can also Suppress other people's negative behaviour and prevent it from raging out of control.

If other people are directing negative behaviour towards you – be it belittling, criticising, getting defensive or any of the behaviours I outlined at the start of the chapter – then there's a good chance you're triggering them with your communication style. Remember, not everyone thinks like you and not everyone places the same importance on the things that you value. It's perfectly OK and normal for some people to be triggered by your communication style. It's not OK for them to exhibit negative behaviour towards you. When they do so it can create a difficult situation for you, so it's up to you to choose: be a victim or Take ownership of the situation.

There are three ways to respond to negative behaviour: you can choose to not acknowledge it; you can call out the behaviour later or you can call out the behaviour in the moment. I'll look at each of these options in turn, but first, let's bring back our friend PLEASE from Chapter 1.

Using PLEASE to defuse the situation

When negative behaviour happens, there's auto-matically a conflict. Assuming the other person is the perpetrator, they're clearly unhappy and if you're on the receiving end you're not going to be happy either. As soon as a conflict occurs, get going with PLEASE.

The other person will have stated the Problem either directly (they've stated what's wrong) or indirectly (they're angry/annoyed so clearly something is wrong). There'll be something deeper going on, so don't respond to negative behaviour with your own negative behaviour. Show some empathy and with-hold your judgement. You may find this difficult, but whatever you do, don't fight fire with fire. Two wrongs don't make a right and your relationships will suffer as anyone that witnesses this may become scared of you themselves. Winning the battle is irrelevant if you lose the war.

Let's say Henry is sitting down with Jennifer, one of his designers, who's briefing him on her latest deliverables. There's a big presentation to a grumpy stakeholder tomorrow and Henry (as usual) feels he has to deliver it as Jennifer would get too bogged down in the detail. Henry is unaware that Jennifer has learnt some new skills about taking ownership of dif-ficult situations.

Henry: (in an irritated voice) 'Right, what have you got for me and what do I need to present tomorrow? I'm really busy so don't do your usual thing of giving me all the background spiel. Just tell me what I need to know.'

Jennifer: 'OK, I can do that. I think you'll be really pleased with what the team has created. Before I show you though, just checking... You seem a bit annoyed.'

Henry: (even more irritated) 'Look, I'm fine, can we just crack on with this?'

Jennifer: 'Sure, I can do. Although if there's something I've done to upset you, it would really help me to know what it is.'

Henry: (calming down a bit) 'You haven't done anything. I'm just really busy and this presentation is the last thing I need.'

Jennifer: 'It sounds like you've got a lot on your plate.'

Henry: (much calmer) 'I do, but it's OK. I'll make it work. This presentation has to go well.'

Jennifer: 'I'm obviously going to brief you on the designs now. What else can I do to help with the presentation?'

Henry: 'I honestly don't know. I've tried telling your team not to get bogged down in the details when you're presenting, but it doesn't seem to happen. I'd love to get some help preparing for this, but I can't deal with another presentation that doesn't go down well. There's too much riding on this.'

And just like that, Jennifer has helped Henry calm down and get to the nugget of the Problem. Going forward, they can now work together to collaboratively come up with a win-win outcome. Notice how Jennifer didn't make Henry wrong for being rude to her and she didn't demand an apology. She chose to not call out his behaviour and instead gave him space to work through what was stressing him out in a non-judgemental way. Now we've reminded ourselves of PLEASE again, let's explore the three options for responding to negative behaviour:

Option 1: Don't call out the behaviour

The majority of negative behaviour is mild and a one-off. In these instances, just use PLEASE to get to a good outcome. The other person will likely thank you at the end and you might even get an apology (but don't sweat it if you don't).

There are two other instances when you shouldn't acknowledge negative behaviour being directed at you.

The first is if you're being triggered by someone else's communication style. For example, you might feel that you're being rushed into making a decision, or conversely, that your efforts to push through a decision are being held up. In these instances, you need to change your mindset – the others are as valid to feel the way they do as you are. The second is if you're triggering the other person with your communication style and you recognise this (well done, you). In this instance, just change your behaviour, ideally apologise and move on.

Option 2: Call out the behaviour later

If you feel there's negative behaviour being directed at you and it's happening regularly, then you should call it out. Avoid challenging the other person in the moment. Imagine if Jennifer had called out Henry at the start of their conversation when he was still irritated; it wouldn't have gone well.

Instead, work through the PLEASE framework with them and Suppress any of your own negative behaviour due to you feeling upset or angry. Remember, they likely don't mean to be rude – there's a deeper issue at stake here. Once you've finished with PLEASE and reached a win-win outcome, you can call out the behaviour by starting a new PLEASE process. Here's how Jennifer might do this:

Henry: 'I'm glad we've had this conversation. I feel a lot better about the presentation tomorrow and it's good to have your help.'

Jennifer: 'Great. Would it be OK if I talked to you about something?'

Henry: 'Sure.'

Jennifer: 'It's about the way you talked to me at the start of the conversation. I totally get that you've got a lot on and that you feel you need to do all the presentations yourself. That's really hard for you. At the same time, I don't respond well to be spoken to in the way you spoke to me. What do you think?'

Jennifer has stated the Problem (the way Henry spoke to her) and is now ready to Listen, Explore and collaboratively come up with a solution. Henry will (hopefully) not be talking to her in this way again.

Where possible, try to avoid challenging someone's behaviour in front of a group. Your chances of getting a positive outcome are reduced with an audience, as they're far more likely to get defensive. If need be, book a follow-up meeting with them to talk through the negative behaviour. There may also be occasions where you think you should call out the negative behaviour, but don't feel you're able to. For example, if you're on the receiving end of a senior stakeholder's ire, then you may enlist your manager to call out the behaviour on your behalf.

Option 3: Call out the behaviour in the moment

On rare occasions, you'll want to stop the conversation dead in its tracks to call out the negative behaviour that you're experiencing. This isn't ideal as the other person is still trying to Solve the problem they're facing and their emotions are high, so they're likely not in a receptive place. You should only do this if the negative behaviour is *really* bad and/or personal and needs to be stopped. Imagine if Henry hadn't calmed down in his conversation with Jennifer and was continuing to be rude to her. Here's what she might say:

Jennifer: (in a calm voice) 'Hold on, I need to stop you, Henry. I totally get that you've got a lot on and you feel like you need to do all the presentations yourself. The way you're talking to me right now does not work for me.'

Henry: (really annoyed) 'I don't care, I haven't got time for this.'

Jennifer: (still calm) 'I'm afraid I'm not OK with anyone speaking to me like this. I'm going to get some fresh air and then let's continue this in fifteen minutes.'

Once again, notice how Jennifer isn't making Henry wrong and isn't demanding an apology. Instead, she's attempting to start another PLEASE process about the way that Henry is speaking to her. Hopefully Henry will have calmed down in fifteen minutes and they can go through the process to come up with a win-win outcome.

There are other occasions that you might want to call out the behaviour in the moment. Maybe you won't get the chance to talk to the person later, in which case you may need to act now. Also, if the negative behaviour is being directed at people in your team and you're more senior, you may wish to step in to show that you've got their backs and to make it clear to everyone that the behaviour is unacceptable.

Ideally, you'll always Take ownership of difficult situations. However, if the situation is caused by a senior stakeholder or a stakeholder that seems to thrive on intimidating other people, you may not be able to. In these instances, you'll need to get going with Empathising and assuming the best of intentions, and Reframing for strength and resilience.

Empathise and assume the best of intentions

The Babemba tribe in Southern Africa has a truly unique way of dealing with bad behaviour. If someone in the tribe commits a crime or a misdemeanour, everyone else forms a circle around that person. They don't punish them, or beat them or shout at them. Instead, they take turns to tell the person all the great things they've done over the years, going into lots of detail. This goes on for a really long time as everyone in the tribe has to speak. At the end, they have a big celebration and the person who behaved badly is then symbolically welcomed back into the tribe.[5] Even though this person has committed some kind of misdemeanour, everyone still assumes they have the best of intentions and they all focus on the positive impact of their contribution to the tribe.

Everyone you work with has the best of intentions the vast majority of the time. In fact, almost everyone you meet in your life has the best of intentions most of the time. The wise folk in the Babemba tribe have realised this and show compassion unconditionally.

Whatever way someone operates in your presence, be sure to judge them by their intentions and not the behaviour. If you're not sure what their intentions are, what's driving them or what's causing them to be annoyed, just ask. A simple question like, 'You seem really annoyed – what's going on?' will often do the trick. They'll likely appreciate the opportunity to offload. No matter how unacceptable you find the behaviour, you must look beyond this to uncover the true intentions. Remember, their negative behaviour is not being directed at you personally, even though it may feel that way. It's being directed at a suggestion you've made, something you've done or the situation you're in.

A Harvard Business Review study found that rudeness at work leads to 48% of people decreasing their work effort, 66% saying that their performance declined and 78% of people reducing their commitment to the organisation.[6] Don't be part of these statistics. If you shift your judgement to the other person's intentions then it's amazing how empowered you'll feel, how much less the situation will affect you and how much better your relationships will become.

Creating psychological safety

Psychological safety is the belief that there won't be any negative consequences for anything you may wish to say – including questions, opinions, suggestions and mistakes you've made.

If Jennifer chooses to judge Henry by his behaviour, then she's going to have a wholly negative experience with him in this conversation. She'll carry that burden around with her for the rest of the day, and ultimately, into future conversations with Henry. If he ends up being rude again, then their relationship goes on a downward spiral. She's the victim; he's the perpetrator and no one's happy.

Alternatively, Jennifer can judge Henry by his intentions. Objectively, he does seem to work hard for her team and tries to get other stakeholders onboard to the designers' ways of working. Thinking he has to do all the presentations himself is another example of him trying to get other stakeholders to buy into her work and he's certainly better at schmoozing senior stakeholders than she is. Immediately, Jennifer is starting to appreciate Henry's intentions. With some good Listening and Exploring, she can work with Henry to find a good solution for both of them. Henry is more senior than Jennifer, but she's still stepping up to manage the situation so they both win, and their relationship can flourish.

The key thing here is that Jennifer is showing empathy to Henry. While his behaviour isn't OK, he doesn't mean to be rude to her and his intentions are good. By focusing on his intentions, Jennifer can create psychological safety for Henry and help him channel his positive intentions into more positive behaviour. She may call him out on his negative behaviour later if she thinks it's appropriate. Hopefully she won't need to, as there's a good chance he'll apologise.

Conversely, if she makes Henry wrong, then he won't feel any psychological safety. His behaviour is unlikely to improve and if he feels backed into a corner, it's likely to get worse.

Reframe for strength and resilience

Henry is clearly stressed out and taking it out on Jennifer. This isn't right or fair and Jennifer shouldn't accept being a victim of it. Perhaps he's doing it because his boss is putting intolerable pressure on him to deliver something that everyone knows isn't achievable. Perhaps he had an argument with his partner that morning about who was going to pick up their child as their nanny was sick. Maybe he has a major deadline tomorrow and doing this presentation is the last thing he needs as he's up against it with the deadline.

Jennifer could create a story that Henry just doesn't like her and she's the victim. She could pick any of the above stories, or any other story. The thing is, all these stories are as valid as each other because – and here's the key thing – she just doesn't know. If someone at work is annoying or frustrating you, then you're the one that ends up carrying the emotional burden, not them. Multiply that burden by the ten other times people have upset or annoyed you, or by 100 times, or by 1,000 times… Well, then it becomes a major burden.

How reframing helps

Reframing is a brilliant technique that helps you create alternate conclusions and stories from difficult events. Jennifer could absolutely use reframing after her challenging conversation with Henry to help her rationalise what happened (and to make sure she doesn't cede to being a victim of his behaviour).

As humans, we tend to take every experience we have and turn it into a story in our minds. You create your stories and these are unique to you. This also means you have the power to change those stories and Reframe your perspective.

It's impossible to have a strong relationship with another person if you're a victim of their negative behaviour. You'll feel tense every time you see them and you're unlikely to perform well when they're around. Reframing helps you make different conclusions from difficult events. You'll end up judging people by their intentions and not their behaviour; in turn empowering yourself to look for these opportunities. Bring this into your everyday routine and you'll feel happier, more energised and more motivated at work (and in your home life). In turn, your impact and performance will increase.

Get a reframing buddy

Reframing is less effective if you just try and process the thoughts in your head (although this is a good start). Remember, you're only 10% likely to do something if you only think about it and 65% likely to do it if you commit to someone else.

Unless you're willing to pay for a qualified leadership coach, you should ideally get yourself a reframing buddy so you can coach each other. You'll also learn a lot by helping them, as well as the help they give you. You should meet your reframing buddy on a regular basis. Meeting up once a week is a good start but you can always meet more or less frequently – whatever works best for you. Agree upfront roughly how long you'll each have to do your reframing. Just get the first session booked in the diary. Assuming it goes well, you'll likely want to keep it going.

Not sure how to broach the subject with a potential reframing buddy? Show them this chapter and get a conversation going. You may be surprised at how open other people are to this kind of thing. Your buddy can be someone you work with (as long as you generally like them), a peer in a different organisation or anyone that understands your job and the challenges you face day-to-day.

How to do reframing

There are lots of different techniques for reframing. Now you've got your reframing buddy, let's take a look at three reframing techniques you can use to get started:

1. Give yourself advice from someone else

Imagining yourself getting advice from other people is a straightforward and powerful coaching technique to reframe a negative experience (or an upcoming challenge). Think about one of those negative experiences and imagine that you went on to resolve everything. In fact, over time, everything went according to plan and you've got exactly the outcome you wanted.

Your future self then jumps into a time machine and comes back to give you advice. What do they tell you about what happened? What's their advice to you? What do they suggest you should do? What else do they tell you? Explore what they have to say in depth. If you're doing this with your reframing buddy, they should keep asking you questions about the different things your future self is saying. Once you've finished exploring what your future self has to say, talk about what you're going to do next.

Instead of using your future self, you can also use a 'hero' of yours, someone you admire and respect and who you think would know how to get out of this situation.

2. Brainstorm what you should be grateful for

Henry was rude to Jennifer (again), but it could have been worse, right? He could have criticised her for the quality of her work. He could have shouted at her in front of her team. He could have made her work late to redo all the work that she'd done.

Henry could have insisted that Jennifer does the presentation to the grumpy stakeholder, who she finds intimidating. Maybe Henry decides that design is no longer important and he stops fighting for her team's ways of working within the business or perhaps later in the day she's told there are cutbacks and she's being made redundant.

So yes, Henry was rude, but the overall situation could have been way worse. Whenever you have a difficult experience, spend some time taking a bigger picture view of the situation. Talk through what else is going on and what you can be grateful for. For example, Jennifer might be grateful that although Henry is generally rude, he doesn't ever criticise her work and he does try hard to sell it into other stakeholders. She might be grateful that he's dealing with the grumpy stakeholder and she doesn't have to. She should definitely be grateful that he's so good at schmoozing senior stakeholders. She likes the organisation and the work she does, so she's certainly grateful for her job. And so on.

Once you've explored your reasons to be grateful, come up with the top three and then reflect back on your situation again to compare your original conclusions of the situation with your new ones.

3. Use scaling to work out how to improve things

Jennifer might score her working relationship with Henry a five out of ten. While he can be rude to her, there are certainly worse situations that she can envisage. Can she also envisage a better working relationship with Henry? What might a six look like? What would need to happen to push it to a seven, or even an eight out of ten? Scaling is a great way to start thinking about incremental improvements and what you can do to make each one happen.

For Jennifer, a score of six might be that things are the same, but Henry isn't rude to her. She knows how to use PLEASE, so this is certainly in her control. A score of seven might be that they work collaboratively on presentations, so she'll need to work out how she can make that happen.

In summary

The six stages to building strong relationships are:

- **M**ap out people's communication styles
- **A**djust your communication style accordingly
- **S**uppress your negative behaviour
- **T**ake ownership of difficult situations
- **E**mpathise and assume the best of intentions
- **R**eframe for strength and resilience

Get M and A right and you'll achieve win-win outcomes in more of your conversations. Even with you

Adjusting your communications, negative behaviour can sometimes creep in, so use S and T to combat this and drive a positive outcome. When this isn't possible, use E and R to recover and come back stronger.

It's quite easy to put elements of PLEASE into action straightaway. It takes a bit more time and introspection to become a relationship MASTER. If you're doing a self-retro as you go along, remember to write up a list of 'What I do well' and 'What I can do better' against the key points for building strong relationships. Here are some to get you started:

❑ Start noticing how people react to your and other people's communications. For negative reactions, assess what happened to have triggered these.

❑ Write down a list of what you think your negative behaviour is and share it with a few trusted people. Have them hold you to account on improving this.

❑ When someone behaves in a negative way, focus on their intentions and not their behaviour. Always ask yourself where they're coming from and what they're trying to achieve.

Grab a handy copy of these and a summary of the best practices in this book at www.humanpoweredbook.com/resources.

Building up strong relationships is the second part of the six-part model in this book. Once you're in a good place with managing conflict and creating strong relationships, you can elevate yourself at work by starting to lead and influence everyone around you.

THREE

Grow Your Influence With Empathetic LEADership

Leadership is no longer about command-and-control

Fred was the leader of one of the world's largest banks. He had a meticulous eye for detail so couldn't believe it when him and his fellow executives were served pink wafers during a meeting. Pink wafers. So tacky. The staff that served the pink wafers were threatened with disciplinary action. Fred ruled with an iron fist. That was OK; it meant people would obey him and were more likely to focus on achieving the targets he set for them. He interrogated his senior management team every day and openly questioned their competence in front of each other. In 2008, the government bailed out RBS to the tune of £20bn and Sir Fred Goodwin was forced to resign his role as CEO. His rage about the pink wafers became infamous. Sir Fred is one of the last bastions of a dying breed of leader, one obsessed with power and control. For him, creating an environment of fear was important: if you want results, the stick is more effective than the carrot.[7]

Companies born in the digital era have created a new operating model, and with it, a new type of leadership. These businesses have pushed decision-making authority from a small number of senior executives down to staff at all levels across the business. In short, everyone is empowered to be a leader, think for themselves and proactively contribute to the organisation's success. There's plenty of data to back up the effectiveness of this. Companies listed in the Glassdoor Best Places to Work have outperformed the rest of the stock market for many years and companies with high employee engagement have been shown to achieve higher profit and productivity than those without.[8] This is why an increasing number of businesses are adopting this new way of working and new style of leadership.

Even the US Army has realised that command-and-control isn't generally effective. According to General Stanley McChrystal, in Afghanistan the officers would tell the troops that 'when you get on the ground, if the order that we gave you is wrong then execute the order that we should have given you.'[9]

What is leadership?

For businesses to succeed, we all need to be leaders. We should show leadership to people in our immediate teams. We should show leadership to other stakeholders across the business. We should show leadership to the leaders in the business. Yes, this includes you, however senior or entry-level you may be. Leadership is no longer based on hierarchy. *Leadership is getting people to perform to the best of their abilities while driving towards a shared goal.* This is a really important sentence, so please re-read it and then let's pick it apart.

As leaders, we're all responsible for getting other people to perform to the best of their abilities. You won't find the path to success by focusing solely on your own goals. You might get a few quick wins doing this, but eventually people will cotton on that your only concern is for yourself. Why would they bother helping you if you don't help them? In a world of matrix structures, we're interdependent. You're far more likely to tread the path to success if you go out of your way to help other people succeed. If we all proactively help one another to succeed, then we all win.

Provided that everyone's goals are generally aligned (which in principle they should be), then driving towards a shared goal is usually possible. By helping people succeed, you're helping them to achieve their goals. You'll likely have to use PLEASE a lot to achieve win-win outcomes that fulfil everyone's individual goals as well as the shared goal.

We all have a leader within

You don't have to be a tyrant to be a leader (phew). You don't need to be superconfident (many great leaders aren't). You can have imposter syndrome (many leaders do). You don't need to be the loudest person in the room (the best leaders listen a lot more than they talk). All you need to do is help other people perform to the best of their abilities while driving towards a shared goal. How you choose to communicate and what leadership style you use is up to you.

At the core of effective leadership is empathy. If you score high in empathy then you can understand what other people are feeling, look beyond their external behaviour to their true intentions and demonstrate that you understand them. All these are essential base ingredients for helping other people raise their performance. If you don't score high for empathy then don't worry – this whole book is more or less an extended 'how to' guide for developing empathy, so keep reading.

As well as having lots of empathy, there are specific tactics you can use to show strong leadership and influence stakeholders. That's what the rest of the chapter is dedicated to.

LEADership framework

The PLEASE and MASTER frameworks generally show you how to react to certain situations. Got a conflict with someone? Use PLEASE. Got a communication challenge with someone? Use MASTER.

LEADership, on the other hand, is all about proactive behaviour. Leadership is proactive by nature. If you need to influence people in your team and stakeholders across the business, then you'll need to:

- **L**ook for the basics and get these right

- **E**stablish great rapport

- **A**mplify your impact

- **D**elight stakeholders continuously

Do all this, mix in a large dollop of empathy and a genuine desire to help everyone succeed and your influence will soar as you show strong leadership to the people around you.

Doing great work is only half the battle in garnering influence. You also need stakeholders to *think* you're doing great work. Many stakeholders don't understand (or care about) the ins and outs of your craft, so they rarely judge your performance on the intricacies of your deliverables. Yes, you read that correctly. The things you spend the most time doing and which are clearly the most important to you aren't the things you get judged on most of the time. They're often not the things that will get you that promotion or pay rise or increase your influence either.

You may want to talk in depth about what you've been working on, the process you went through and what you've delivered. After all, you've been head down, working in the reeds for a while. The thing is, many senior stakeholders lean towards the Director and Socialiser communication styles, so they're often far more interested in the outcome of your work rather than the detail – specifically, how what you've done will have a positive impact on their goals, the business and customers.

So, read on to find out what you can do so people *think* you're doing a great job and you can influence with ease.

Look for the basics and get these right

When it comes to leadership, a lot of people forget about the basics. Do so at your peril. If you don't get the basics right then you quickly eradicate trust and goodwill. Along with empathy, the basics are the base on which you build your leadership and influencing skills.

It's (almost) impossible to over-communicate

In marketing, the Rule of 7 says we need to hear a message seven times before we'll take action.[10] The Mere Exposure Effect tells us that people will only get familiar with a message when they're exposed to it 10–20 times. You develop a preference for something merely because it becomes familiar.[11] If you need to communicate something to persuade people to do, think or feel something as a result, then you need to tell them repeatedly and ideally across multiple channels. It's (almost) impossible to over-communicate.

If there are issues that might cause you to miss a deadline, flag this immediately to the relevant stakeholder. If you don't get a timely response, then follow up to check that they received your message. Keep communicating updates over time so they always know what's going on. Whatever you do, don't send a message out once and then have an attitude of, 'I've told them now so it's their fault if they don't do anything about it,' when you get no response. You're responsible for the outcome, not just sending the message.

The same applies to deadlines. Continually and vocally remind stakeholders of deadlines (and the consequences for missing them) in meetings, in follow-up group emails, in one-to-one team chat messages, etc.

Listening to yourself repeating the same thing may get boring to you, but you're using empathy here.

This means thinking about things from the other person's perspective, and the other person needs to hear your message multiple times for it to sink in. You're the same when people tell you things.

You can, and likely often do, under-communicate. It's (almost) impossible to over-communicate.

Don't leave them hanging

When you're physically speaking with someone, feedback is instant. You say something, they respond and so on. When the conversation is moved to email or team chat, there's a lag between what you say and the other person's response.

As a general rule, commit to responding to messages from your most important stakeholders within three hours. You'll never be in a meeting or doing deep work for longer than this without a short break. Even if your response is just to acknowledge the message and say you'll get back to them tomorrow by lunchtime, that's fine. Don't leave them hanging.

Then make sure you do actually respond by lunchtime the next day, because that's what you said you'd do. You always do what you say you'll do by when you said you will, right? If you're not ready to respond by lunchtime the next day, send a message to tell them this (with an apology) and that you'll now send a response by the end of the day.

Don't let people think you don't care

Making other people realise you care is more or less covered in the E, A and D parts of LEADership. You also need to stamp out behaviour that makes other people think you *don't* care about their needs.

To start with, you must be ruthlessly on time for everyone else's meetings. That's right: ruthlessly. Without fail. Not one minute late. Being regularly late for other people's meetings is a classic example of negative behaviour. Repeat offenders often do this to exert power, albeit subconsciously (refer back to Chapter 2 for more on this). You don't want to get a reputation for this.

You'll always make sure your meetings run to time (well, you will after you've read the next chapter on facilitation), but other people's meetings can overrun to make you late for your next meeting. If there's a risk of this happening, tell the meeting organiser upfront, or at least send a quick message as soon as you know you might be late. It's OK to do this every now and then – just don't make a habit of it.

Be fully present in other people's meetings. Don't check your phone. Don't answer a call just to say that you're in a meeting and you'll call them back. Don't check email. Don't get distracted and look around the room. If it's a virtual meeting, stop being distracted by other applications you've got open. When you start reading something and stop fully listening, your facial expressions noticeably change. If you wear glasses, everyone can see you switching windows as it reflects in your lenses. All of these are negative behaviours, and you're going to struggle to influence people if you don't respect them enough to be present in their meetings.

If you don't think you need to be at a meeting, then politely decline it and state why. Better still, ask the question first to check if it's worth attending, as you might have misunderstood the meeting's purpose. Don't turn up late and sulk because you've got better things to do. If you're super-busy, then tell this to the meeting organiser beforehand. Tell the organiser that you're still committed to supporting them and get a PLEASE process going to come up with a good outcome. (In this case, the Problem is that you're now too busy to attend the meeting but you still want to help them succeed.)

When it comes to your own meetings, just being on time isn't good enough. You need to be ready at least ten to fifteen minutes before start time, having ruthlessly prepared for it. That's right, ruthlessly. Have you:

- Defined the meeting objective and shared an agenda?

- Checked that you've got all the correct cables for the AV and tested them all?

- Confirmed that the sound works for the video you'll be playing?

- Pre-opened all the files you're planning to show?

If you're doing a virtual meeting, are you comfortable with the different software features you'll be using? Are you able to share your screen while still looking at your notes and watching everyone's videos? If you're meeting face-to-face, have you gone into the room before the meeting to tidy up, clean the whiteboard and check the markers work?

Everything you don't check is something that can go wrong, and that causes your meeting participants to wait while you sort it all out. A few minutes of wasted time here and there multiplied by all the people in the meeting soon adds up.

Be sure to thank people for coming to your meetings, regardless of where you each sit in the hierarchy. They've taken the time out to be there, so share your gratitude and share the progress that's been made as a result of the meeting. A bit of positive reinforcement always goes down well.

I'll talk a lot more about facilitating meetings and workshops in the next chapter.

Establish great rapport

You've got all the basics in place and no one thinks that you don't care about their needs. Now let's take this up a notch and start to Establish great rapport.

You'll struggle to Establish rapport if you hide behind email or team chat. Face-to-face (in person or virtual) works far better. In fact, research cited in the Journal of Experimental Social Psychology found that face-to-face communications are a whopping thirty-four times more successful than emails.[12] Thirty-four times!

Please, start actually *talking* to stakeholders. The more rapport you have with people, the more likely they are to trust, support and listen to you. The more they do this, the more likely they are to help you achieve your goals. In short, if you take the time upfront to Establish great rapport, your working life will become better and easier and you'll save time and frustration.

Email and team chat are great for setting up and summarising face-to-face conversations (in person or virtual) and team chat is especially effective for trivial communications. They're not at all effective for dealing with anything nontrivial. Being thirty-four times less effective than face-to-face communications, written communications should be avoided as much as possible. (There is a place for written comms which I'll tell you all about in Chapter 6.)

PLEASE be a MASTER

You'll struggle to build rapport without following everything in Chapters 1 and 2. People really like it when you actively Listen. They like it when you Explore what they're thinking as it helps them process their thoughts. They like it when you create psychological safety for them to speak openly. They like it when you proactively ask them what their concerns are.

Most people also like it when you stand up for yourself (a key tenet of the Articulate part of PLEASE). They'll generally respect you more for it and know that, while you'll do what you can to help them succeed, you won't do it at the expense of not succeeding yourself.

People also like it when you Adjust your communications to suit their style. They'll enjoy talking to you as the conversation will work well for them. People like being with others that always think the best of them, Empathise and don't make them wrong. Remember, many senior stakeholders are Directors and Socialisers when it comes to communication style. They're far more interested in the outcomes you're going to help them achieve and far less interested in the work you've done and how you're getting there.

In short, follow the PLEASE and MASTER frameworks and you're well on your way to Establishing great rapport.

Be curious so you can create connections

A Harvard University research study used MRI scanning to track brain activity during conversations. When people felt that they were talking to other people with similar interests and beliefs, the ventromedial prefrontal cortex lit up. In short, we get happier when we're with people that we think are like us.[13]

There are three ways to find out more about the people you work with: do some online research, ask other people about them and ask them directly.

When meeting a new stakeholder, you should always do some online research before you meet them. Check the internal systems to see who they report into, who reports into them and work out what their objectives are likely to be. Look them up on professional sites or social media. Where have they worked previously? What are their interests? Where did they grow up? What university did they go to? Doing appropriate research on someone you're meeting is not unusual and they'll usually appreciate you taking the time to get to know them before you meet.

If the person you're about to meet has worked with colleagues you already know, ask your colleagues what the person is like and find out a bit more about them. Your colleagues will generally like doing you a favour and long-term this can help you (also known as the Ben Franklin effect – more on this below). You should also ask questions when you meet. If you've done your research then you can do this from a position of knowledge. Asking questions, being curious and having a genuine interest in the answers is a good thing. People generally like to talk about their own beliefs and opinions – doing so activates the regions of the brain that are also responsible for the thrills of food, sex, money and drug addiction. That's right, talking through your perspective can be as rewarding as food, sex, money and drugs!

Remember Chapter 2 though – people with different communication styles have different priorities. Relators and Socialisers will likely be open to personal chat as soon as you meet. Directors and Thinkers usually want to crack on with the task at hand, so the beliefs and opinions they share will likely be related to what they're working on and will come out more sporadically. In short, encourage people to talk about themselves as much as they want to, but don't force the issue.

Once you've let them talk about work or their personal life (ideally with you showing empathy and actively listening), then it's your turn to start talking. Choose something they've said that you can identify with and share your thoughts. Open up and be genuine. If you can, show some vulnerability. This is great for building rapport, encourages the other person to do the same and shows that there's going to be psychological safety in your relationship. If all else fails and you both have kids, then just talk about them. Everyone can relate to the joys and challenges of parenthood.

The more you get to know them, the more you can find things in common and the more you'll Establish rapport. If you don't ask questions then it's difficult to form a connection. After all, how can you find things in common with another person if you don't take the time to find out more about them?

Here's how a first conversation might go with Sarah, a senior stakeholder new to the business, and Peter, a product manager:

Sarah: 'Hi Peter, nice to meet you.'

Peter: 'Nice to meet you too. Welcome to the company. I saw on LinkedIn that you were previously at Acme Inc. for the past five years.'

Sarah: 'Yes, that's right. I really enjoyed it there.'

Peter: 'A friend of mine used to work there. He says it's a great culture.'

Sarah: 'It really is. It was a hard decision to leave.'

Peter: 'I'm curious, what was it about the culture that you liked so much?'

Sarah: 'They were generally really supportive. There was a strong no-blame culture which resonated a lot with me.'

Peter: 'It sounds like you fitted in really well there.'

Sarah: 'Yes, for sure. I'm going to miss that place.'

Peter: 'I'm really pleased you mentioned the no-blame culture. I'm not sure we're as strong on that here, but it's something that's important to me. I work hard to maintain a no-blame culture with my team and the benefits are obvious to me.'

Sarah: 'That's good to hear. I've been a general advocate of this for a while now.'

Peter: 'Yes, I read your blog post about not assigning blame. I liked the way you described how you ran your retrospectives. Maybe you can tell me more about these another time? I think I could learn a thing or two from you.'

Peter has clearly done his homework. Before even meeting Sarah, he's worked out some of the things they have in common and has steered the conversation to these topics. First impressions really count and their relationship has gotten off to a great start.

Put other people's needs ahead of yours

Imagine that the Queen is coming to your house. How might you host her? How might you behave in her presence? Take a moment to think this through and then think how you might apply your answers to your meetings with team members and other stakeholders.

Your day-to-day actions (or inactions) will build trust (or break it down), so take the time to get these right. Always open the door for other people, beckon them to go first, offer them the first biscuit, don't pour a drink for yourself without offering one to them first, don't bring in a drink without having first offered them one and so on. In short, put other people's personal needs ahead of yours and proactively think about how they can be as comfortable as possible.

Also ask permission a lot, especially if you want to say or ask something that could be contentious. 'Do you mind if I challenge you?', 'Can I ask you a really blunt question?' and, 'Is it OK if I'm direct with you?' are all great ways of getting a stakeholder to opt in to hearing what you're going to say. Doing this manages their expectations, prepares them to be challenged and gives them ownership of this part of the conversation.

Remember the Ben Franklin effect

Ben Franklin, one of the eight Founding Fathers of the USA, once quoted what he called an old maxim:

'He that has once done you a kindness will be more ready to do you another, than he whom you yourself have obliged.' Now referred to as the Ben Franklin effect, psychologists believe we tell ourselves that we help others because we like them and it would feel weird to do a favour for someone that we don't actually like.[14]

Amplify your impact

Not being good at your craft makes it difficult for you to Amplify your impact. Unfortunately, the opposite isn't true. Being good at your craft is just expected and is unlikely to increase your influence by itself. Remember, the skills that you might value the most (ie being good at your job) are rarely what you're judged on by stakeholders across the business. By now you're Looking for the basics and getting these right and Establishing great rapport. Next it's time to build on these and start influencing and persuading stakeholders, so you Amplify your impact.

Create the right first impression

According to a Harvard University study, it takes eight positive encounters to overcome a negative first impression, so any time you meet a new person, make sure they know how great you are and how great the people in your team are.[15] Have your personal credentials ready at all times, as well as those of your team members.

You can also send these credentials over to introduce yourself and the team beforehand and then use them as part of your introductions when you meet. This isn't about boasting or giving yourself an ego trip. It's about making sure that stakeholders understand what you're capable of and what you can do for them.

Your personal credentials should be short. No more than five or six lines. They should start with the outcomes you deliver (not the intricacies of what you do day-to-day), explain why you're an expert and say something about what you're passionate about. You should be able to substantiate everything you say and it should all pass the 'Opposite Test'.

'I'm a hard worker', 'I'm committed' and 'I have a good attitude' don't pass the Opposite Test because no one would ever say the opposite of these. Can you imagine anyone saying, 'I'm not a hard worker', 'I'm not committed' and/or 'I have a terrible attitude'?

When Peter met Sarah for the first time, he shared his credentials as part of his introduction:

> 'I empower my team to create products that
> our customers love and which drive genuine
> business benefits. I integrated user research
> into our sprint cycles last year and help other

product managers do the same. I'm a realist and know we can't always do what's best for users as we have to balance this with commercial realities. It seems to be working: over the past year, my product has helped increase conversions by 5%. I love my product manager role as there's so much variety. No two days are ever the same.'

Notice how he substantiates his successes, passes the Opposite Test throughout and ends on what he's most passionate about. I want Peter to be my product manager when I read that. When you meet new stakeholders, you need to introduce yourself properly. Be sure to also get them excited about the future by sharing stories of previous successes and obstacles you've overcome. Storytelling is really important here (Chapter 5 is dedicated to this).

Don't try to persuade people

If you want to persuade someone to take on your point of view, going all out to persuade them isn't always the best idea, especially if you have a win-lose attitude. Besides, your opinion may not actually be correct.

Refer back to everything you've read in Chapter 1 about conflict resolution, and instead use PLEASE to try and get a win-win outcome. During a PLEASE process the other person can sometimes have a strong viewpoint which they're struggling to see past. In this instance, you can get them to use self-verification to alter their beliefs during the Explore stage. Resist the temptation to impose your opinion. Instead, get them to challenge their belief themself and then you can gently ask questions and put forward your perspective. You'll start by asking a question that encourages them to take an extreme version of their viewpoint. They'll likely then start backtracking from the view and be more open to an alternative view.

For example, if an engineer often doesn't put new code into a shared code library (they're too busy) then you might ask, 'Shall we just get rid of the code library altogether?' If a product manager makes their own changes to the prioritisation list after you've already had a planning meeting, you might ask, 'Would you prefer it if we stopped doing the planning meeting altogether?' Perhaps a senior stakeholder insists that the work you've been doing isn't in line with what they want. You might ask, 'Would it be better if we downed tools while I try and put a new team on this?'

To reduce the chances of coming across as aggressive or passive-aggressive, be sure to ask permission before asking questions like these. For example, 'Can I ask you a really blunt question?' Assuming you get an affirmative response, follow this up with, 'Are you sure?' The double opt-in is a good way to get them ready for the main question. Most of the time, they'll start backtracking and you can gently get them to collaborate towards a win-win outcome. Occasionally, they might actually say yes to your outlandish question. While this isn't what you intended to happen, it isn't necessarily a bad thing. Your question isn't what prompted them to say yes; they were already feeling this way. Far better for them to discuss their thoughts with you than for them to go away and make their mind up on this without doing so. In the unlikely event of this happening, just start a PLEASE process. The Problem is they're suggesting that something happens which you don't want. Follow the process and you can hopefully resolve it with a win-win outcome.

Don't ask for what you actually want

If there's something that you want, start by asking for much more or for much less. These are known as the door-in-the-face and foot-in-the-door techniques respectively. You're three times more likely to get what you're asking for if you use one of these techniques, according to research published in the *Journal of Personality and Social Psychology*.[16] That's correct, you triple your chances of getting what you want, so read on.

If you ask for what you want straight off the bat, the other person will likely be unprepared for the request. They need time to get used to the idea and to process it in their mind. Just asking outright, no matter how reasonable a request it seems to you, can make them feel like you're putting them on the spot. They may feel they need to provide an instant answer, and it may not be what you want to hear.

Let's look at the door-in-the-face technique, so called because if you're a door-to-door salesman and you ask for an outrageous price for a simple product, you're likely to get the door slammed in your face. Imagine if our product manager, Peter, is running behind schedule for a crucial launch and needs three additional engineers for two weeks. The Problem is that when he's asked before, he's often been refused and been told the team should be managing their time better (even though he'd pushed back at the start and said that the timelines were unrealistic). He could send this message to Sarah on team chat, sit back and wait for a response:

> 'As I mentioned a few weeks ago, the timelines for this launch aren't realistic given the team size. We've got two weeks to go and the only way we can make this happen is if we have three more engineers working on this or the launch will be delayed.'

Hopefully you remember what you learnt in Chapter 1. You should never engage in conflict resolution with a written message, so sending this on team chat is a bad idea. The way it's written also gives the impression that Peter is more interested in protecting himself than seeing the launch succeed. This is never a good idea if you want to Amplify your impact. Instead,

Peter should be using team chat to set up a meeting with Sarah. Remember, he's more likely to get a good outcome face-to-face anyway (thirty-four times more likely), so instead, he writes:

> 'It's obviously two weeks until launch and I'm 100% committed to hitting this deadline. At the same time, I'm concerned we're not going to make it. Please can we meet ASAP to discuss options for making sure we meet the launch deadline? It looks like you're free at 9am tomorrow morning if that's good for you?'

Much better. Peter hits send and meets with Sarah first thing the next day. He goes through the PLEASE process, trying to coach her to come up with a solution (he's already read Chapter 1). They're in the Solve part and Sarah hasn't been able to come up with a solution yet, so he decides to use the door-in-the-face technique:

Peter: 'OK, so the only other thing I can think of to make this happen is if we get six more engineers on the team to support us.'

Sarah: 'What? We don't have that kind of resource available and there's no budget left anyway.'

Peter: 'OK, that clearly doesn't work.'

Sarah: 'No, not at all.'

Peter: 'Hmm... Do you mind if I challenge you a bit on this?'

Sarah: 'Sure.'

Peter: 'I totally get there's no more budget. The thing is, once we go live, this product will generate millions each year. Is there really no way we could get a bit more money? The business will see the return almost immediately.'

Sarah: 'I don't care. We're already over budget and I'm not willing to go back and beg for more money.'

Peter: 'Yeah, fair enough. That would be an awkward conversation. There's obviously a lot of pressure on all of us to get this live.'

Sarah: 'Yes, there is.'

Peter: 'Hmm... What if we could get just three engineers supporting us for the next two weeks?'

Sarah: 'I might be able to make that work. I thought you needed six?'

Peter: 'We do. I'm thinking though... We could push back the latest change request until after launch as we can easily go live without it. Our designer also does front-end development, so I could get her helping out with coding as there aren't any critical design changes that need doing. If we do both of these, I reckon we'd only need three additional engineers.'

Sarah: 'Interesting. I think I could make that work. Let me check with one of the other teams. They're not working on anything high profile right now so I'm pretty sure I could get them to give you three of their engineers for two weeks.'

Peter: 'Great.'

Having originally said no, Sarah then said yes to the second and comparatively reasonable request. Peter got what he needed and Sarah feels good about it. Best of all, it was a constructive meeting that cements their good relationship. Sarah may be more senior than Peter, but she's already appreciating the way he empathises with her and his can-do attitude.

The door-in-the-face technique is best if you need a decision straightaway. It's really effective with people that like to make quick decisions (ie Director and Socialiser communication styles – see Chapter 2 for a reminder of these). If, on the other hand, you need longer-term decision-making and/or commitment, the foot-in-the-door technique is best. This involves asking for much less than what you actually want and then gradually asking for more over time. It's a great technique to use if you want stakeholders to come on the journey with you by gradually getting them to agree to larger commitments over time.

This technique also gets its name from door-to-door salesmen. In this instance, getting someone else to keep agreeing to do something is akin to keeping your foot in the door so it can't be shut on you. For example, you might want a particular stakeholder to join your daily stand-up for thirty minutes each day. You need their regular input to make sure you're delivering in line with expectations, but they're really busy and you're pretty sure won't be willing to do this.

Start by asking for a small commitment – perhaps just five minutes each day at a time that suits them. Assuming they say yes, do this for two to three days and then ask to increase this to fifteen minutes, explaining why doing so will benefit them. As they've already said yes once, they're more likely to say yes again. After a few days, if the fifteen minutes doesn't seem long enough, then suggest an increase to thirty minutes and again explain the benefits to them.

When someone says yes to a small request, they're far more likely to say yes again to a larger request. Doing so means they're being consistent with their original decision, something that people generally like to do.

Have a can-do attitude

You'll also Amplify your impact if you respond positively and generally have a can-do attitude when things go wrong. Things often don't go according to plan and your reaction in these instances is important.

Step up to take responsibility for what's happened and ownership for helping to make it right. Taking responsibility builds trust and accountability and people around you will respect you for doing so. Taking responsibility is not the same as taking the blame.

Criticising others is an example of negative behaviour; doing so rarely reflects well on you and typically diminishes your impact. If someone hears you criticising or blaming other people, who's to say you're not going to criticise or blame them when they're not around? You can focus your energy on pointing fingers or you can focus your energy on trying to resolve the situation and get to a positive outcome. I know which person I'd rather spend time with.

Remember Peter's original message on team chat? His sole objective was to protect himself so he wouldn't get blamed. He didn't send this message in the end, and his other message and communications in the meeting showed he was fully committed to a positive outcome.

Delight stakeholders continuously

I've explained how to Look for the basics and get these right, Establish great rapport and Amplify your impact. Now it's time to start motivating people so their performances increase and they work harder to achieve your shared goals. It's time to Delight stake-holders continuously.

Do solve problems but don't make decisions

Assuming there's a shared goal and everyone knows the direction of travel, there are always problems that need solving and obstacles that need overcoming along the way. You'll Delight stakeholders if you continually help them clear the path ahead. To do so, you'll need a curious mindset (so you can fully understand the problem) and a can-do attitude (so you're determined to find a solution).

You don't need to come up with the solution each time, but you should always offer ideas and facilitate the conversation to help generate potential solutions. You won't Delight stakeholders or teammates if you just tell them what the problem is, ask everyone what they'd like to do and then wait for them all to make a decision. You don't need to be the loudest person in the room, but you should engage in the conversation with suggestions, exploratory questions and examples of when you've seen similar problems being solved.

When it's time for decision-making, don't push anyone into a corner to get them to choose what you think is the correct option. (You've read Chapter 1, so you know not to do this.) Let's say there are two potential ways forward: Options A and B. You strongly feel that option A is best. Simply explain the advantages and disadvantages of each one (of course, option A will have a lot more advantages than disadvantages) and then say to the decision-maker, 'But you are free to choose.'

You'll double the chances of them agreeing to option A if you use the 'But you are free' technique.[17] Even though you're relinquishing decision-making and aren't pushing hard for them to agree with you, you still double the likelihood of getting your way. By giving ownership of the decision, they have time and space to reflect on your arguments and don't feel pressured to make a decision. After telling them that they're free to choose, let them explore their thoughts. There's a good chance they'll pick the right option. If they don't, well, so be it. You may not actually be correct. (Shock! Horror!) You've put your arguments across for why option A is best but you didn't force the issue and that's a good thing. Even if you tried to force your opinion through, there's a good chance they would have chosen option B anyway.

By not forcing the issue, you've created psychological safety for the person making the decision (psychological safety can go up or down the hierarchy). This means that if option B turns out to not be the best choice, they're less likely to stick with it to save face and more likely to speak with you about reverting to option A. If you had tried to force through option A and failed, your relationship would likely have been damaged. Your relationships with people that witnessed your behaviour may also have been impacted if they didn't like what they saw.

Tell everyone what a great job they're doing

As soon as you start working with stakeholders and new team members, go out of your way to provide positive feedback to everyone, no matter where they sit in the hierarchy. This isn't about sucking up or blowing smoke where the sun doesn't shine. It's about being aware of the positive intentions and behaviour that someone else is exhibiting and telling them that you've noticed.

Provided your feedback is genuine, specific and fact-based, it's impossible to give too much positive feedback. Phrases like 'Great job', 'Good work' and 'Well done' are meaningless and can actually reduce your impact. Great job on what? Good work with what? Well done about what?

Your feedback should mostly be about intentions and effort. If the outcome is good then do mention this, but feedback that acknowledges intentions and effort is more fulfilling than feedback that focuses on outcomes. Good examples of positive feedback might look like this:

- 'I know we didn't get where we wanted, but I really appreciated your support the whole way. I felt like you had my back and every time I asked for your help you were quick to give me what I needed. When our key stakeholder kicked up a fuss, I don't think I could have overcome that without your coaching.'

- 'Wow, look what we've achieved. This will have a great impact on the business and I hope we're all recognised for that. Regardless, I really enjoyed working with you. You challenged my thinking a lot and that worked well for me. By working together, we've ended up with a better product than I could have created by myself.'

- 'I want to acknowledge the effort you've put in to finishing this. I know you've been working long hours and I want to say thank you for sacrificing so much of your personal time this week for the launch. We've spoken previously about you not always being committed and that's not the case here at all. Your commitment has been amazing.'

These examples are providing feedback up the hierarchy, to a peer and down the hierarchy respectively. Positive feedback can flow in any direction. You'll usually use it to praise good intentions and/or behaviour. You can also use it to praise someone who's no longer exhibiting negative behaviour, as per the last example. This is great for reinforcing the progress they're making and the effort put in.

Positive feedback can also just be in the form of a simple 'Thank you' and an explanation. For example, if

someone tells you something that's in any way contentious then they might have been nervous about
doing so. A good response that you can use to anyone
in the hierarchy would be something like: 'Thank you,
I really appreciate you taking the time to tell me that.
It's not always easy to say these things but by getting
it out in the open, we can talk about the best way forward for us both.' Positive feedback can also be in the
form of a celebration of success. Whenever things go
well or your team has achieved a milestone, initiate a
celebration. The scale of the celebration should be in
line with the scale of the success.

In our constant push to keep driving things forward,
we rarely remember to provide positive feedback to
those around us. Make this a regular part of your routine and more people will want to spend time with
you and help you achieve your goals.

Make other people warm to you

People like it when you proactively think about their
needs. It shows that you understand them, you want
them to succeed and you're thinking about what they
need. If you don't know what your stakeholder's
objectives are, just ask. How else are you going to best
support them if you don't know?

Do one proactive activity per week for each of your
key stakeholders to support them in achieving their
objectives. For example, do a web search to find

relevant articles, blogs and TED Talks in line with their objectives. Send them a link to one of these and explain why it's relevant. As a team, brainstorm what concerns or questions they may have each week and proactively allay these potential concerns by answering the questions. Your goal here is for stakeholders to never ask you a question or state a concern as you're always second-guessing what they need. You're unlikely to achieve this goal in reality, but do strive for it.

It's the little things that count here. Keep doing these regularly and you'll build lots of trust over the long-term.

Also use people's names a lot in conversation. Dale Carnegie, who wrote *How to Win Friends and Influence People* says that, 'A person's name is the sweetest sound in any language for that person so hearing it validates our existence, which makes us more inclined to feel positively about the person who validated us.'[18] If you're meeting with people you haven't met before, be sure to write down their names in the order that they're sitting, as a reminder.

Finally, if you and your team are working hard then make sure stakeholders know just how much effort you've put in. If you've all been working twelve-hour days in the run-up to launch, it's important that stakeholders know this. People are busy and often don't look up to see you putting in the extra effort. Don't be shy to share the fact that you've gone above and beyond, or how will they know you've worked so hard to help achieve the shared goal?

In summary

You can and should be showing leadership to everyone around you, regardless of where you sit in the hierarchy. I've outlined four components for leading and influencing:

- Look for the basics and get these right
- Establish great rapport
- Amplify your impact
- Delight stakeholders continuously

Think of these as building blocks. Start with the best practices covered in L and once you've got a solid foundation in these, work your way through the rest. There's no point trying to Delight stakeholders if you're getting all the basics wrong. If you're doing the self-retro, start with the L guidelines and work your way through the rest of the framework, in order, writing up what you do well and what you can do better against all the best practices.

By the way, none of this works unless you're genuinely curious about other people and want them to succeed. You can lean on all the techniques in this chapter to manipulate people, which will help you in the short-term, but people will see right through you in the long-term and these techniques will generally stop working. Instead, use these techniques to create win-win outcomes and to make sure everyone succeeds and they'll serve you well for a long time.

In terms of next steps, I suggest that you:

❏ Write a list of the L best practices you should start doing. Take a few weeks to work through your list, consciously putting it all into practice.

❏ Write your personal credentials. You should always have these to hand, ready to introduce yourself to anyone in the right way.

❏ Experiment with putting one technique at a time into practice, starting with E and then working through A and D.

Within the LEAD framework there's no one big thing you can do to have a large impact; it's a collection of lots of best practices. It takes time for new behaviour to become habitual, so stick at it and within a few months you should see real change in how people behave towards you.

You're now halfway through the six-part model and you've learnt how to resolve conflict, build up strong relationships and lead and influence people. You can use these skills in all aspects of your job (and your personal life).

Next up, we'll look at facilitating meetings and workshops. You'll need all your new skills to do this, as well as doing some specific things which I'll outline in Chapter 4. Let's get READY for that now.

FOUR

READY, Set, Go Facilitate

Meetings are often ineffective

You've got a big meeting coming up. You sent out the invitation weeks in advance. You've checked and it's in everyone's diaries so they should all know to attend. If they need to know what it's about, they can see the agenda you've conveniently attached to the calendar invite.

The big day comes about... and only two people turn up on time. Most of the others come along a few minutes late. No one seems to fully understand why they're there (which makes no sense as you sent them the agenda). As the meeting progresses, people just don't seem to be that interested or engaged in what you want to talk about. You're trying to get a discussion going, but one of the senior stakeholders (who everyone knows is too opinionated) keeps going off on tangents. It's like they only want to discuss things that aren't on the agenda. The meeting finishes and you're not quite sure what to do next. You weren't 100% sure what you wanted from the meeting in the first place and now you're no further forward in your thinking. Oh well, at least it was good to get people together and it seemed like people enjoyed meeting up to chat.

According to the Journal of Business and Psychology, almost 80% of people say meetings that they initiate are productive, yet only 56% say the same about meetings initiated by others.[19] There's a clear disconnect here. When we run meetings that we think are great, the people attending often disagree.

The cost to businesses of ineffective meetings is vast. Imagine a one-and-a-half-hour meeting with five people that doesn't achieve its objectives. That's one-and-a-half hours lost for five people. Add that up and you've lost an entire working day for one person. Multiply that by every ineffective meeting and the cost to the business becomes significant. There are some other damning statistics about meetings. In a study conducted by Atlassian, 91% of people said that they daydream in meetings and 73% admitted that they use face-to-face meetings to get other work done.[20] These stats are likely to be even higher for virtual meetings.

It's really important that your meetings and workshops are effective

Over time, people learn whether your meetings and workshops are well run or not. Do you fail to provide a written agenda or have no clear purpose for your meetings? Do you turn up unprepared? Late? Distracted? Do you allow your meetings to go off on tangents? Instead of holding meetings, could you have communicated via team chat or another internal tool? If the answer is yes to some of these questions, you'll start getting a reputation for not running useful meetings and workshops. If this happens, getting people to emotionally commit to your events becomes difficult, no matter what you do.

Your interactions with everyone you work with affect your reputation, and many of these interactions will be in meetings. Calling a meeting is a true test of your reputation. Nowadays, managers seem to spend the majority of their time in meetings, so finding time to actually get their work done can be a challenge. Waste someone's time for an hour and they'll likely remember.

Maintaining a good reputation internally is key to job success. The better your reputation, the more likely people are to support you in achieving your goals. This makes it more likely that you'll achieve your goals, which in turn enhances your reputation. It's a virtuous cycle. If you run highly effective meetings and workshops, people are more likely to think highly of you and support you. If you get a reputation for holding inefficient and ineffective meetings that waste people's time, well, the opposite comes true.

READY framework

The READY framework is the blueprint for running successful meetings and workshops. Follow the best practice guidelines and your meetings and workshops will be efficient and effective, that is, they'll achieve their objectives in the quickest possible time.

The READY framework explains what you should do before your meeting or workshop (R and E), during (A and D) and afterwards (Y):

- **R**esponsibility for the meeting success is with you

- **E**motional commitment – get everyone choosing to attend

- **A**ssertively lead the room

- **D**rive everyone to the outcome

- **Y**ou are accountable for all action items

Responsibility for the meeting success is with you

Before you even start to get READY for a meeting, think long and hard about whether you need to have one.

Your reputation is on the line with every meeting you set up, so make sure it's worth it. Remember, the total time spent in a meeting is the meeting duration multiplied by the number of people attending. According to research carried out by multiple universities, we also get 22% less work done in the hour before a meeting as our minds start to get distracted, and it then takes twenty minutes to get back into our tasks once the meeting is finished.[21] Your meeting costs your business time and money, so in the interest of organisational success make sure you truly do need to meet.

How do you decide whether you actually need a meeting? Ask yourself whether using team chat, email or an internal system would be more effective than getting everyone together. Generally speaking, using any of these is better than meeting up if:

- The objective is for you and / or others to inform or share

- It's likely that only one person will have actions

- It's a simple, fact-based discussion about an uncontroversial topic

On the other hand, meetings are usually appropriate if:

- Your objective is for people to solve a problem

- It's likely that many people will have actions

- It's a complex debate about a contentious topic, with multiple stakeholders and/or with high levels of subjectivity

Some people also prefer having meetings. Remember the different communication styles from Chapter 2? People whose dominant style is Socialiser (and to a lesser extent, Relator) can find it difficult to engage with written discussions, especially if the two of you don't have an existing relationship. You'll need to Map out their communication style (as per Chapter 2) to work this out.

Outcome first, agenda second

If there's only one thing you're able to communicate to people before your meetings, choose to share your target outcome. Most people think to put together an agenda and will often share this upfront. Most people also forget to mention the outcome they're trying to achieve. In fact, many people don't even consider what outcome they'd like from the meeting.

If you can't work out what your target outcome is, then don't have a meeting. Creating your target outcome is relatively straightforward. Simply finish the sentence, 'When everyone leaves the meeting, I want them all to…'

For example, 'When everyone leaves the meeting, I want them to…':

- Fully define the problem that needs solving, and all its facets.

- Agree on our priorities for the next three months.

- Put me in line for a promotion and pay rise.

- Buy in to what's in scope and out of scope for the upcoming launch.

- Reach consensus on the product vision and long-term roadmap.

- Understand each other's roles more clearly and what everyone is trying to achieve.

Once you've defined the target outcome, you can put together the meeting objectives, who you should invite and the agenda. Make sure that all of this maps back to the outcome. When you start to invite people, be sure to share the target outcome with them immediately. Ask for their feedback so you can see if there's misalignment on what people want to get out of the meeting. If there is, either adjust your target outcome or suggest that a separate meeting take place.

With a clearly defined outcome, you can rein in people like your opinionated senior stakeholder so they stay focused and on track during your meeting. Before they attend, they'll know why they're there, and if they do veer off-topic you can remind them of the target outcome. (I'll give you some tips on how to do this later in the chapter.) Once the target outcome is agreed, you can put together and share the agenda.

For simple, non-contentious meetings with a short lead time, you might send out the target outcome and agenda at the same time.

Check in on how you did

You should make a habit of getting feedback on the effectiveness of your meetings, especially for important events. It's pretty easy to put together, and respond to, a simple feedback form asking for a one to five rating of the meeting's effectiveness and one thing that could have been better. Realistically, many people won't respond, but the comments in the responses you do get can be invaluable.

Make it efficient

Remember, the people you work with are generally time-poor, so they'll appreciate your meetings being as efficient as possible. Getting a reputation for running efficient meetings is a good thing. Be sure to organise logistics well in advance and double-check everything beforehand. For face-to-face meetings, make sure the room booking is in place, the room is stocked with whiteboard pens and there are cables to hook up your computer, etc. For virtual meetings, double-check the tech works in the way you think it will and test everything. This is all basic stuff but don't overlook its importance. (Take a look back at

Chapter 3 for more on Looking for the basics and getting these right.)

As well as getting the basics right, you can make your meetings efficient by carefully choosing the invite list and assigning pre-work.

Carefully choose the invite list

Once you know the target outcome, invite the absolute minimum number of people needed to achieve it. The fewer people you invite, the more each individual is able to participate. The discussion becomes richer, more in-depth, inclusive and intimate, so it's more likely that people will speak openly and candidly. It's also far easier for you (the facilitator) to manage the room and steer the conversation towards your target outcome. There's a balance to be had here. Your meeting won't be effective if certain stakeholders aren't present, so choose the invite list carefully.

If you need people from a particular team to attend, ask the team leader which one person you should invite to come along and relay the discussion back to everyone else in the team. Don't invite the entire team for fear of offending or just in case people want to attend. Your objective here is to make your meeting as efficient as possible and the more people that attend, the more you reduce the chances of this. If some people only need to contribute to a small part of the discussion, do this part first and then allow them to leave the meeting.

If you feel that people need to observe the discussion so they understand the decision-making, don't invite them. There are other ways to achieve this outcome without forcing them to sit through the meeting. For example, you can record the meeting and they can watch it back in their own time, or you can include them on messages you send out after the meeting (more on follow-up messages below).

Assign pre-work

There have been a number of research studies to show that individual brainstorming ('brainwriting') is more effective than group brainstorming. There have also been plenty of studies that show the opposite is true. To achieve your target outcome, you should ideally do both. Get people to come up with suggestions, ideas and/or thoughts by themselves (ie brainwriting) and also have group discussions. The former can be achieved by assigning everyone pre-work before the meeting. Pre-work is particularly useful if you're going to have a complex debate with high levels of subjectivity about a contentious topic.

During meetings people can get passionate about their ideas and emotions become raised. This makes it difficult for them to think objectively, so it's important that pre-work is structured and gets everyone to think objectively about their ideas. People might enter into the pre-work with preconceived ideas, but if you ask the right questions, you can help them to think objectively.

If you're holding a meeting to discuss prioritisation, you might get everyone to do pre-work to choose their top three desired features and write down:

- Why these features are best for users.
- How the features will add the most value to the business ahead of other ones.
- Concerns they have for launching these features and what could go wrong.

If your meeting is to gather requirements, you might get stakeholders to write down three business objectives they'd like to see supported.

If you have a meeting to get stakeholder sign-off for a new feature, you could ask everyone to write down:

- Their top three concerns for the new feature.
- Their top three basic requirements.
- Their top three dream attributes of the feature if time and money were no object.

If your meeting is to review progress so far, well, do you actually need a meeting for this? (Caught you out there!) The simple, uncontroversial parts of any review can often be done without having a meeting. If things then start to get contentious, set up a meeting.

What if you can't get people to actually do the pre-work? Always plan for this to happen (it often will) and make sure you've got a five-to-ten-minute buffer in the schedule for everyone to do this at the start of your meeting (yes, it's OK to have a meeting where you're all writing in silence). Pre-work greatly helps people to Emotionally commit to your meetings and to cite their concerns (which you'll often ask about in pre-work questions).

Emotional commitment – get everyone choosing to attend

A rational commitment is something you agree to. Invite people to your meeting and, assuming they accept your invitation, they've made a rational commitment. Get them to emotionally commit and you significantly increase the chances of your meeting being successful. Emotional commitment taps into people's 'why'. If someone emotionally commits to your meeting, they know *why* they're attending and they deeply buy in to this reason. Get this right and facilitation becomes so much easier. Get it wrong and you may face an uphill battle from the first minute of the meeting to the last.

Create excitement before your meeting

It should be a given that you send out an invite and agenda for your meetings – important, but definitely not exciting.

For every person you're inviting, put yourself in their shoes and ask yourself, 'What's in it for me?' How will achieving the target outcome benefit that person? If it's a stakeholder you don't know too well then ask around: what are their key objectives, what are they trying to achieve in their job and what kind of person are they?

Once you've worked out what's in it for everyone, personalise your invite message to highlight the unique benefits to each person. In reality, there'll be plenty of overlap so you'll rarely need more than two to three versions of your invite message. For routine and informal meetings, you'll usually only need one version of the invite message.

Be sure to sound excited in all your pre-meeting comms. If you're not excited then there's no way they're going to be, so don't write this: 'I'd like to invite you to a prioritisation meeting to get your input on what we should be doing for the rest of the year. I've attached the agenda.'

This is better: 'Let's get together so we can all agree what features to launch this year. I'm keen to learn what your priorities are so we can support you in achieving your objectives. There's just a few of us attending so it should be a productive meeting.' (I'll talk more about written skills in Chapter 6.)

Get your pre-meeting comms right

Don't send over an invite and assume that the other person is genuinely committed to your meeting's success just because they accept it.

Depending on the lead time for the meeting, as well as its importance, you should send out two to four pre-meeting messages. Most meetings are routine and informal so you'll only need two messages. For your important meetings that have lots of people attending, a long lead time and/or a lot riding on them, you may want to send as many as four messages before the meeting.

Let's imagine you're booking in a super-important workshop in two to three weeks' time and lots of stakeholders are attending. The first message you send out is basically to share the target outcome, tell everyone the (personalised) benefits of attending and get them excited for the meeting. That's it – short and sweet. You'll then follow this up with your second message, informally asking each person individually if they have feedback on the target outcome and what concerns they have about the meeting.

Your meeting is far more likely to be effective if everyone is aligned to – and buys in to – the target outcome. If someone goes off on a tangent in the meeting, everyone else will know this and you'll likely have their backing when you try to get the person back on track, so try to get everyone to comment on and acknowledge the outcome beforehand. Getting people to offload their concerns before attending also drives Emotional commitment. People's concerns will naturally come out in the meeting, often not through what they say, but through their behaviour. They can be disengaged, get defensive, criticise other people, turn up late and so on (ie exhibit lots of those negative behaviours you read about in Chapter 2). If people do have concerns, get a constructive conversation going with them before the meeting so they feel good about attending. The PLEASE process in Chapter 1 is what you'll need here.

Once you've gotten agreement on the target outcome and allayed any concerns, it's time to send out your third message. This time, you should share the draft agenda along with a request for feedback on it. What would people like to add, remove or change to make sure the agenda helps you all achieve the target outcome? This is also a good time to assign pre-work. You should send out your third message a week or so before your super-important workshop. If you send all this out much further in advance people are less likely to engage as the meeting isn't really on their radar yet. Be sure to check when people are on holiday, and send it earlier if individuals will be away in the run-up to the meeting.

Finally, send out your fourth message the day before. Remind everyone what the target outcome of the meeting is. Also tell them what the first activity/topic is and the benefit of taking part in this. Your meeting will be more successful if everyone arrives on time, so this is a nice way of trying to make that happen.

You can integrate the foot-in-the-door technique from Chapter 3 throughout your pre-meeting comms, where you gradually ask for larger commitments. For example, in your first message you can ask everyone to accept your meeting invite (requests don't get much smaller or simpler than that). Then move on to getting people to give feedback on the target outcome, contribute to the agenda, do the pre-work, etc. The more they do for the meeting in advance, the more Emotionally committed they become.

You should send out all four of these messages in the run-up to your most important meetings that have a long lead time. Remember, the vast majority of your meetings are routine and informal, so you can reduce your pre-meeting comms to two messages most of the time. Your first message will share the target outcome, ask for concerns and will likely include the agenda. You should always send out a reminder the day before too, and this might include the agenda if you haven't already sent this out. Remember to sound excited throughout all your pre-meeting comms. You want people to Emotionally commit and your excitement can become infectious.

Acknowledge everyone's opportunity cost

There are lots of research studies to quote regarding the importance of effective meetings. One from the University of North Carolina states that 65% of people said that meetings keep them from completing their own work, 71% said that meetings are unproductive and inefficient, and 64% said meetings come at the expense of deep thinking.[22]

Everyone is busy and everyone has an opportunity cost of attending your meeting. There's always something else they could be doing instead. Try to find out everyone's opportunity cost and acknowledge what they're giving up. You can do this by asking them outright in your pre-meeting comms, or for people you don't know well, asking around as to what they're working on.

People that are stressed out about their other priorities can often unwittingly disrupt your meetings. Stress can create an overload in cortisol which can wear down the brain's ability to function properly. It can shrink the prefrontal cortex (the area of the brain responsible for memory and learning) which literally diminishes their ability to socialise with others.

If you have time, and assuming it feels appropriate, get everyone present at the start of your meeting by giving one reason they're excited to be there and one reason they don't want to be there. The reason they don't want to be there is their opportunity cost and you can then get agreement on what to do about this. Let's say Brad is kicking off an important meeting and it's Ruby's turn to share why she's excited and why she doesn't want to be there.

Ruby: 'I'm excited to be here because I want to contribute to the success of this launch. I don't want to be here because I have a presentation to the executive board this afternoon and it's not quite finished.'

Brad: 'Well, first of all, thank you so much for coming along when you have that meeting coming up. Secondly, what do you need from me and the rest of us to make sure you're ready for your presentation?'

Ruby: 'I'm not sure. I've got the rest of the team working on the presentation right now. They'll message me when they've finished and then I can review what they've done.'

Brad: 'OK, great. It sounds like things are progressing. I'm guessing you'll need to keep checking messages during this meeting and you might need a few minutes to look through everything they've done?'

Ruby: 'Yes, I think so.'

Brad: 'Not a problem. Please do that and just let me know when you need to pop out to review their work. I can rejig things a bit to make sure you're still able to contribute to each part of the meeting. What do you think?'

Ruby: 'That sounds great. Thank you.'

Brad has handled this situation really well. He's granting Ruby (a stakeholder more senior than him) permission to do what she needs to do so as to reduce her stress levels. She may leave the meeting for a few minutes, which isn't ideal and he's used up a few minutes of his meeting to have this conversation, but this is all far better than having her stay the whole time while being super-stressed and potentially disruptive.

On another occasion, Ruby might have told Brad that she needs to leave. Not at all ideal, as her input is needed to help achieve the outcome. It's still better than having her stay though. If Ruby is so stressed out that she wants to leave when asked about the opportunity cost, Brad probably doesn't want the meeting to go ahead with her there. Using the 'But you are free' technique from Chapter 3 could work well here:

'We can always push this meeting back to next week. We'll have to rework our timelines so the go-live date will probably get pushed out by a few days, or we can work out a way to keep going. What do you think, Ruby?'

Equally, Brad could have encouraged Ruby to take an extreme version of her viewpoint to help her backtrack from delaying the meeting. A question such as, 'Shall we reschedule the meeting for another time, when everyone's next available?' might work, as to do so would potentially delay things by weeks.

Perceived outcome vs opportunity cost

At its core, achieving Emotional commitment is all about having one of those old-fashioned balance scales. On one side of the scales is the perceived outcome. The perceived opportunity cost is on the other side. You want the outcome to outweigh the opportunity cost by as large an amount as possible.

Picture the balance scale. Visualise the outcome on one side and the opportunity cost on the other. Then visualise the outcome getting heavier and heavier and the opportunity cost getting lighter and lighter. The weight of the outcome is pushing that side of the balance scale down and the side of the opportunity cost is rising higher and higher.

Now apply this to your upcoming meetings. Ideally, everyone's perception of the target outcome is far greater than their perception of the opportunity cost. Spend time making the scales balance in your favour before your meeting. You'll see everyone's Emotional commitment increase and facilitation suddenly becomes a whole lot easier. The more important the meeting, the more time you should invest upfront to make sure that the target outcome significantly outweighs the opportunity cost.

Assertively lead the room

Our minds wander during 47% of our waking hours (according to a Harvard University study), so you can guarantee that people will get distracted during your meeting.[23] This is magnified with virtual meetings when everyone still has access to email, team chat and anything they're working on. You can reduce (but never eliminate) how often distractions happen by Assertively leading the room.

Get off to a good start

If you have a strong start (and if everyone is Emotionally committed to being there), it's likely that your meeting will go well. Wake everyone up and get them focused with a high-energy start. It doesn't really matter what you do, provided it's an activity somehow related to the target outcome and it involves everyone participating in some way. Getting everyone to share why they're excited to be there and why they don't want to be there can be a good start. Or have them share their three priorities for the target outcome or perhaps their number one concern. You get the idea.

You could get everyone to write down their answers (better still, have them do this as pre-work) and then get them to share what they've written in pairs. Each person can then present what their partner said back to everyone else. Alternatively, get everyone to share in small groups of three to four and nominate one person from each group to share the general group sentiment. If you're running a virtual meeting then use the breakout room functionality if it's available. There are limitless options – do what you think is right and appropriate for the people that are attending.

In short, whatever you do, make sure people can start contributing almost immediately. Don't just go around the group having everyone speak in turn. In reality, most meetings are routine and informal, but make sure the first few minutes set the meeting up in the correct way even for these.

Establish the rules

You may or may not need rules for your meeting. Generally, you're more likely to need rules when you:

- Feel there's a high probability of disagreements.

- Have disruptive stakeholders.

- Are running a meeting with a longer duration.

- Have people that don't know each other too well.

Remember, most meetings are routine and informal so don't usually need rules. The more important the meeting is, the more likely it is that you'll need some rules. You'll need to explain the ground rules upfront and rigorously enforce them. The first time someone breaks the rules, be sure to say something (you might want to use PLEASE) so everyone knows they need to stick to them.

You'll most likely need rules for people's behaviour (especially for virtual meetings). For example, don't interrupt others, don't use your phone during the meeting, keep the conversation focused on the outcome, etc. You could ask the group to generate the rules with you facilitating the conversation. Once you've got the rules defined and everyone knows what they are, talk to the most influential person in the room (often the most senior stakeholder) and request that they help you to enforce the rules. It's extremely likely you'll get a positive response. Suddenly everyone in the room knows that it's not just you who'll keep the meeting on track.

Rules or logistics are low-energy topics so remember to do a quick high-energy activity and then define the rules if necessary. You could (and often should) minimise the time spent on this by sharing a draft set of rules with everyone beforehand and then asking for feedback in the meeting.

Manage 'difficult' participants

Your ability to Assertively lead the room comes into play when you need to manage 'difficult' participants. Notice how 'difficult' is in quotes because there's no such thing as a difficult participant. Remember Chapter 2 where you were told to start Empathising and assuming the best of intentions? You'll need to do a lot of that with 'difficult' participants.

In meetings, individuals can be argumentative, overly dominant, disruptive and so on. You'll have laid out the rules at the start and the most influential person in the room would have agreed to support you with enforcing these. Even so, the 'difficult' participant is busy checking and responding to emails or answering their phone when it rings. Perhaps they're just not participating and facial expressions and body language make it clear they'd rather not be there. At other times they might talk over and even belittle others, clearly trying to get to a conclusion so the meeting can finish as quickly as possible. They might also go out of their way to disagree with the popular view so you're all unable to move on.

The thing is, all it takes is one person to exhibit just one of these behaviours and it can disrupt the whole meeting, bring down the mood for everyone and ultimately stop you from achieving your target outcome. Even in the face of all this, you must always assume the best of intentions and that there's an underlying motivation other than to disrupt your meeting. Something else is at play. Once you've got your head around this, you can begin managing the situation with a handy three-stage approach. Show empathy. Remind them about the outcome. Get permission to move on.

First, show empathy and that you understand. Reflect back, don't make the person wrong and try to establish where they're coming from. You may need to interrupt them to do this. Imagine someone in your meeting keeps insisting that what everyone else wants to do wouldn't work. You might say something like:

> 'Can I just interrupt you for a moment if that's OK? Do you mind? It sounds like you've had some terrible experiences working this way. Really, everything you've said sounds awful and I'm not surprised you think this can't work. While you were talking, I was writing a few notes of what you were saying in our shared document. Can I ask you to review this and add anything you think I've missed?'

They clearly want to express an opinion and are valid to feel that way based on their experiences. Your empathetic response is making this clear and still allowing them to contribute (albeit in a shared document). There may be a bit of back and forth here, where you continue to use your active listening skills. You'll then follow up by reminding the person of the meeting's target outcome: 'Now the reason we're here today is obviously to work out how we'll deliver this product. That's what the business wants us to do, so I'm going to keep us focused on that outcome.'

You're making it clear that, despite the objections, you all need to crack on. Then ask their permission to do so: 'I'm going to move things on to the next activity in the agenda. Does that work for you?'

Hopefully you'll get a yes and you can progress the meeting. The objector might keep labouring their point however, in which case you'll need to start the process again, albeit with a slight difference. As before, start by showing empathy and reflecting back where they're coming from. Remind them again of the outcome and then, in the most assertive voice you can muster, *tell* them that you're moving on. No permission needed this time.

Show people that you care

If people feel that you care about them, they're far more likely to care about you (and therefore be supportive during the meeting). Acknowledging everyone's individual opportunity cost helps massively with this.

Beyond this, people generally have three basic needs during the day: to eat, to drink and to go to the toilet. Make sure your meeting allows them to do all three, especially if you're getting together for more than an hour. Offer breaks every hour or so and announce you'll be doing this at the start of the meeting. For face-to-face meetings, put bottles of water and glasses on the table and provide snacks. If you're together for more than three hours then proactively plan for how people will eat a meal, charge their phones and laptops, write notes, hook up their laptop to the screen, screen share, etc. It's amazing how the little things can make such a difference to people's willingness to support you.

Drive everyone to the outcome

If your pre-meeting comms have been effective, everyone should know what you're trying to achieve in your meeting. Now it's time to make that happen.

Get allies

If you've defined rules for your meeting, you'll have also asked the most influential person in the room to help enforce these. It's time to ask them for another favour. Remember the Ben Franklin effect from Chapter 3? Asking favours is a good thing.

State your target outcome right at the start of your meeting, and follow it up with a simple question like, 'Are you all OK with that?' Hopefully everyone will nod their heads as they all know why they're there. Tell them all that you're going to facilitate the meeting to stay focused on achieving this. Look at the most influential person in the room and ask: 'Would you mind helping me with this? I really want to keep the conversation focused and it would be great to get your support with this, if you're up for it?'

Getting the most influential person on your team is great, but why stop there? When you're setting up the meeting, you could assign particular agenda items to other people to lead the discussion. This is a great way to boost their involvement and interest. The more allies you can bring into your coalition, the better. As the meeting progresses, go out of your way to positively reinforce people when someone says or does something that keeps the discussion moving towards your target outcome. Make sure your praise isn't vague and specifically explain how they're helping the group move towards the outcome.

Make it effective and efficient

Whatever you do, don't just turn up for your meeting and hope for the best. Even for the smallest, most informal get-together, take some time to plan out the agenda and what you'll do to facilitate the discussion at each stage.

Running structured activities is usually best as you can avoid circular discussions and / or groupthink, the latter resulting in bad decisions as the group doesn't challenge individual thinking. Your structured activities should allow everyone to participate and contribute ideas. Many people don't enjoy group discussions or brainstorming and don't feel comfortable contributing, so a mix of brainwriting (individual brainstorming, some of which can be done as pre-work) and group discussions tends to work well. There are literally hundreds of different structured activities you could do in your meetings. Ask around or search online to get ideas for what would work for your particular types of meeting.

As facilitator, you're in charge of getting everyone to the target outcome. You'll need to manage the available time so the meeting doesn't run late, which may mean stopping conversations that aren't aligned to the outcome. You'll need some mechanism for people to pick these up later (eg place the topic in a metaphorical 'parking lot'). If you're really not making the progress you need, take a break and chat with one or two allies to help you work out how to restructure the rest of the meeting to make it more effective.

Finally, as facilitator, do your best to remain impartial and facilitate everyone else having the discussion. People are far more likely to listen to you if you're not trying to sway the conversation in a particular direction. If you do have a strong vested interest, you might be better off asking someone else to facilitate.

You are accountable for all action items

At the end of every meeting, you should all agree on next steps and assign actions. Your behaviour when discussing and following up on these actions can greatly increase or decrease the likelihood of them actually happening.

Actions must always be assigned an owner, which might be you or someone else. The owner is responsible for making the action happen, but as the facilitator, You are ultimately accountable for making sure it's completed. Meetings are a waste of everyone's time if the actions don't actually happen. You should never congratulate yourself for running a good meeting, but you should always congratulate yourself for running a meeting where the next steps are all actioned.

Without a specific owner, your actions are far less likely to happen due to the 'bystander effect'. Basically, individuals are less inclined to help out if other people are potentially able to do so. Make it clear who's responsible for each action and you can avoid this. As well as having an owner, each action should be specific and measurable and have check-in and completion dates associated with it. Establishing a check-in date is important – without one, you don't have permission to find out how people are getting on with their actions before the completion date. Your action list might look something like this:

- Liaise with department head to get sign-off on the plan. (Owner: Ken; check-in date: 19th May; completion date: 24th May.)

- Get additional information from a key stakeholder. (Owner: Judy; check-in date: 21st May; completion date: 31st May.)

And so on. You may want to assign some intangible actions but you'll need to make them specific and measurable. For example, an action to think about something can be made more specific by saying that the thoughts need to be shared in a specific format by a certain date. This is all basic stuff, but well worth a reminder. I see even the most seasoned meeting organisers regularly failing at this.

Get buy-in to doing the actions

The last item on almost every agenda should be to discuss next steps, and it's important you do this during the meeting. Don't fall into the trap of wrapping up the meeting and saying you'll send over the actions. You will send them over *and* you'll discuss them there and then in the meeting before everyone leaves.

You'll need to lead the discussion and go through the list of follow-up actions. Start by getting agreement on the owner (sometimes it's obvious who this should be and at other times you'll need someone to volunteer). Next, agree the check-in date and completion date for each action and then spell out why the action is important. It may seem obvious to you, but it's not always obvious to everyone else.

As well as stating why it's important, you should also talk about the implications of the owner not following through on the action. For maximum likelihood of people following through on actions, you'll need a bit of carrot and a bit of stick. Your actions list might now look something like this:

- **Liaise with department head to get sign-off on the plan.**
  Why? To secure budget for the additional headcount.
  If it doesn't happen: We won't have enough engineering resource to launch the feature on time.
  (Owner: Ken; check-in date: 19th May; completion date: 24th May.)

- **Get additional information from a key stakeholder.**
  Why? To make sure we have the requirements for our first sprint in June.
  If it doesn't happen: We'll have to delay the sprint and ultimately the entire launch.
  (Owner: Judy; check-in date: 21st May; completion date: 31st May.)

Once the actions are all assigned, it's still not time to end the meeting. For each action, check in with the owner that they're OK with the dates and confirm they understand why it's important and the implications for not doing it.

Then, it's pre-mortem time. Ask each action owner what the opportunity cost of them doing this action will be, and what other priorities might prevent them from being able to do it. Get them to explore the reasons it may not happen, and once this is done, what they, you and everyone else can do to help mitigate against this. Getting all this out in the open greatly increases the chances of the action happening.

No matter how little progress you've made in your meeting, allow time at the end to discuss actions. The purpose of your meeting is always for actions to happen afterwards. It's generally better to have concrete actions based on you getting partway through the agenda than for you to get through the full agenda and to have ineffective actions.

Monitor progress and provide unconditional support

Every time you book in a meeting, make a habit of blocking out time in your calendar immediately after the meeting. This is when you'll do your follow-up. You'll have discussed the actions in depth in the meeting and now it's time to get this all written down. You'll hopefully have gathered some momentum in the meeting so keep this going by getting the action list out within thirty minutes of the meeting.

There are two follow-up messages you should send.

The first confirmation message goes out to everyone and is the action list. State all of the actions and for each one, why it's important, implications of not doing it, the owner, check-in date and completion date. You discussed all this in the meeting and now you're confirming it in writing and everyone can see what everyone else needs to do. Don't forget to thank everyone for attending. Remember, everyone has an opportunity cost for attending your meeting. It's important to acknowledge that people took time out of their schedule to support you.

Next, you'll send out individual messages to each person that has an action. Confirm that you'll follow up on the check-in date and tell them that you're here to support them. Encourage them to get in touch with you if there's anything they need to help make the action happen, or any challenges along the way.

By sending out both group and individual messages, there's both group and individual accountability. The group is aware of everyone's actions and you've made it clear to the individual that you'll follow up on the check-in date.

Be true to your word and check in with everyone. Adjust the frequency with which you check in based on their communication style (remind yourself of these in Chapter 2) – generally, Relators and Socialisers are more focused on relationships so will likely appreciate you reaching out; Directors and Thinkers who are more focused on solving problems, less so. For the latter groups, only reach out when you say you will. If anyone is struggling to complete their actions, or simply not doing anything, you'll need to get going with a PLEASE process. Don't make them wrong for their inaction. Use your empathy skills to find out where they're at and come up with a win-win solution. For everyone that's completing their actions, or making good progress, make a big thing of this and positively reinforce this behaviour (regardless of where you both sit in the hierarchy). As always, make your praise specific, focus on the effort made and explain the impact their behaviour is having.

Avoiding other people's ineffective meetings

As I mentioned in Chapter 3, if you're not sure you need to attend a meeting then (after checking that you understand the meeting purpose) politely decline and state why. Don't succumb to FOMO (fear of missing out) and don't accept every meeting invitation. If a few people from your team are invited to a meeting, have one person go along and get them to send a summary around to everyone that doesn't attend.

Skipping unnecessary meetings will free up your time, and if you do everything I'm suggesting in this chapter, you'll need extra time to prepare properly for your meetings and then take accountability for all actions. It's well worth it though; your impact, effectiveness and reputation at work will soar.

In summary

When it comes to running successful meetings and workshops, you need to get READY:

- **R**esponsibility for the meeting success is with you

- **E**motional commitment – get everyone choosing to attend

- **A**ssertively lead the room

- **D**rive everyone to the outcome

- **Y**ou are accountable for all action items

The success of your meeting or workshop is only in part down to how you run it in the moment. What you do before (R and E) has a major sway in how effective it is, and can set you up for success or failure. While your actions after the meeting (Y) won't affect how well it goes, they will affect the impact of your meeting and whether or not you achieve your target outcome.

If you only do three things after reading this chapter, I recommend that you:

❑ Always focus on the outcome. Everything follows from your target outcome, so make sure you clearly define this for all your meetings.

❑ Appreciate the opportunity cost. Find out what the people you invite could be doing instead of joining you.

❑ Stop attending so many meetings. You need time to prepare for and follow up on your meetings.

You can put these three points (and any of the other best practices) in the 'What I do well' and 'What I can do better' sections of your self-retro. We're so often judged by our performance in meetings rather than our performance at doing our jobs. Use the best practices in this chapter, as well as everything I've outlined in the previous three chapters, and those judgements will likely be good ones.

You'll of course need to speak in your meetings (whether you're the facilitator or not) and the next two chapters will show you how to do so effectively. In Chapter 5, in particular, I'll be showing you how to create DRAMA through storytelling.

FIVE

Storytelling With DRAMA

The power of storytelling

I was once working with a product director called Oliver. I'm in a meeting with him and he's worried about the budget. He's trying to get rid of the user research to cut costs but we're launching a completely new feature so this seems like a bad idea to me. I share a bunch of stats around the benefits of user research but the harder I try and the more I implore him to change his mind, the more I'm getting nowhere. I'm thinking to myself, 'What more can I do here?' and then, a story pops into my head.

I tell Oliver the story about an online application that we redesigned. The application process we created was brilliant, but we still ran user research on the prototype before launching. You know what we found? It was brilliant. We had designed a brilliant application process. Apart from one form field. In our research, no one could understand what to do with this field. If we hadn't been there to explain it to users, no one could have gotten through the process. It took us five minutes to re-engineer that form field based on what happened in the research. When we tested it again with users, it worked well and we launched. If we hadn't done that user research, not one person would have been able to complete an application.

I tell this story to Oliver and you know what happens next? He says, 'OK, I get it, we'll keep the research in scope.' This is the immense power of storytelling.

In Chapter 1 you read how to Articulate your point of view as part of the PLEASE process, in Chapter 2 you learnt how to build up strong relationships and in Chapter 3 you reviewed lots of techniques for leading and influencing people. Storytelling will help you achieve all of these, so it deserves its own chapter. Storytelling is part art and part science, so in this chapter I'm going to go into the minutiae about how to be a successful storyteller.

Storytelling is particularly effective when you're delivering a presentation, as you've got everyone's attention for an extended period of time. That said, it works in almost any situation when you want to influence, lead or build rapport. You can still tell stories if you're in a regular meeting, but you'll likely need to do it more quickly than when you're presenting. You can also tell stories spontaneously, although the best stories are the ones you've told at least ten times. Don't feel like you need to reinvent the wheel and come up with a new story each time. You might feel bored of telling the same story so many times, but your audience neither knows nor cares that you've told the story before. Focus on engaging them, not yourself.

Think about how stand-up comedians (who are basically professional storytellers) go about their craft. They write their script, which is a series of stories, and then test it out a number of times with small audiences. They iterate and adjust it as they go along and once their gags are landing, they then go out on tour. Each night they go through the same set; most of what they say mirrors what they've said the night before. They still put the same amount of energy into it and adjust their tone of voice in line with what they're saying and the emotional state they're recounting. Each new audience is engaged and doesn't feel like the comedian is just regurgitating a script.

Storytelling does things to our brains

Listening to stories affects our brains in a way that regular conversation doesn't even come close to doing. When you hear a story, the neural activity in your brain increases by up to five times. When more of your brain is at work, the chances that you'll remember something increases exponentially. When your brain experiences an emotionally charged event like a story, it releases dopamine. Dopamine also makes it easier for you to remember what you're hearing. You produce oxytocin when you're being engaged with a story. This sends a signal to your brain that you should care about someone (ie the lead protagonist of the story). It creates a level of empathy that wouldn't otherwise exist.

There's a lot of data to back this up. A Stanford University research study showed that statistics alone have a retention rate of 5–10%, but when coupled with anecdotes, the retention rate rises to 65–70%.[24] That's an increase of up to fourteen times. According to research from cognitive psychologist Jerome Bruner, we're twenty-two times more likely to remember a fact if it's told in the form of a story.[25] In short, our brains are hardwired to enjoy and remember stories. This isn't a new thing – the oldest known story in the world, 'The Epic of Gilgamesh', was scribed on clay tablets over 4,000 years ago.

The Hero's Journey

No explanation on storytelling would be complete without mentioning the Hero's Journey story template popularised by Joseph Campbell in his 1949 book, *The Hero With A Thousand Faces*.[26] During his studies of mythology, he found a whole host of similarities between stories told across time and cultures. The most beloved stories all seemed to follow a similar core structure. In short, the Hero's Journey centres around a protagonist (our 'Hero') with whom we have great empathy (which the story creates). We're rooting for the protagonist the whole way through. The protagonist has a call to adventure (which they initially refuse), ventures into a new and unknown world, meets lots of new people (friends and foes), faces a major ordeal which they overcome to achieve their main goal and then (finally) head back home, changed forever.

This core structure is the basis of many of the highest grossing movies of all time: *Star Wars*, the *Harry Potter* series and *Avatar* all follow this structure, as do *The Matrix*, *The Wizard of Oz*, *Finding Nemo*, *Lord of the Rings* and *The Lion King*.

The Hero's Journey can't be used in its entirety in business storytelling (it's far too long and more appropriate for a two-hour movie or a novel), but as it's been the most well-used story structure for millennia, you shouldn't ignore it. You can still use its key elements when you tell stories at work.

DRAMA framework

For most people, getting started with storytelling is the hardest part. How do you know when to tell stories or what stories to tell and where do you even get your stories from? Fortunately, our DRAMA framework helps you to come up with stories and apply a structure to them:

- **D**efine the objective

- **R**ecord the key details

- **A**pply an engaging structure

- **M**agnify engagement levels

- **A**ccumulate your stories

The first four stages are all about putting your story together, and I'll show you a step-by-step process you can follow to do so. The final A is all about how you build up a bank of stories over time, ready to be unleashed in many common situations. Accumulating a collection of stories is a lot more straightforward than you might think.

You'll need to put time and effort into creating your stories. Not as much as a stand-up comedian, but certainly more than you might expect. Remember, the best stories are the ones you've told at least ten times so the upfront investment will eventually be worth it, and as with anything, it'll get quicker and easier the more experienced a storyteller you become.

When you break the process down into these five steps, storytelling becomes accessible to everyone. If you don't do much storytelling, follow my framework to get yourself started. Once you get over the initial hump of uncertainty, it's plain sailing and you'll hopefully be telling stories to influence, lead and build rapport forever more.

Define the objective

As I talked about in Chapter 4, every meeting needs an objective and you shouldn't book in a meeting until you know what this is. The same applies for your outbound comms, which you'll read all about in the next chapter. Don't even start communicating until you've worked out what you want to achieve. This is also true for storytelling. Every story needs to have an objective. Don't bother creating or telling a story until you've clearly Defined the objective. What's the outcome you're trying to achieve? What do you want people to do, think and/or feel after hearing your story? Your objective should run at the heart of your story so that you (and your audience) know where you're headed. For example, your objective might be to:

- Get sign-off on some new designs and/or user journeys.

- Secure additional engineering resources.

- Get an extension to a deadline.

- Agree on future prioritisation.

- Get buy-in to a set of features you're planning to build.

- Keep the research in scope (as with Oliver at the start of this chapter).

When do you, or your team, try to influence stakeholders to buy in to your recommendations? When do you need to define or change someone else's opinion or behaviour? List the times you need to do this. Think up at least three to five common scenarios (some of them might be listed above). These are the situations where you'll want to have stories to hand. Next, for each of your three to five scenarios, think up a time when you or someone else achieved the desired objective. These are your stories. Coming up with ideas for stories is really that simple.

In the story that I told to Oliver, my objective was to change his opinion about removing the research from the scope. Validating design decisions with users can be the difference between a successful and unsuccessful product launch. I had this story in the back of my mind as stakeholders often think to cull research when faced with time and budget pressures.

We tend to overthink and overcomplicate the story ideation process. Most of our experiences seem ordinary to us because, well, they are ordinary. We often don't think it possible to use these as the basis of our stories, but even the most mundane of experiences can be turned into a story if someone achieved the desired objective.

As well as basing stories on your experiences, you may sometimes want to tell a fictional story. This is especially the case if your objective is to get buy-in to, and sign-off on, the work that you've done. For example, to bring your deliverables and the process you went through to life, you might want to tell the story of a typical customer interacting with your brand. You'll still Define the objective upfront, but you'll only be able to think up the story when your work is almost finished and ready to showcase.

Please put this book down for a moment and write down a few examples of when you need to influence stakeholders. Then write down when you've successfully done this against each example, no matter how mundane or ordinary the experience was. Once you've done this, you'll Record the key details, Apply an engaging structure and Magnify engagement levels to create your story. Let's look at each of these three stages next.

Record the key details

Once you know what your story will be about (ie an example of when a particular objective was achieved), hold off writing it. Instead, Record the key details first. The Hero's Journey is arguably the most engaging and familiar structure, so let's take some of the important elements from this and note down the details for your story. There are five key details you should flesh out before starting to create your story, as follows:

1. Who's the lead protagonist and how will your audience empathise with them?

Start by defining who you'll likely be telling the story to. A business stakeholder? An engineer? A product manager? Ideally the hero of your story, your lead protagonist, will be the same type of person facing similar challenges and with similar objectives to your audience. Your audience should be rooting for the protagonist right from the start and you'll increase the chances of this happening if they can relate to and empathise with the hero.

Your hero also needs an objective, a problem that needs solving. Your intended audience should be able to relate to this objective. This means that the hero of the story will often not be you. You can absolutely be a part of the story, it's just that you won't always be its hero. Sorry.

2. Who are the other characters?

To bring them to life, stories should feature a few different people. We need to know who else is present and how they're contributing to the practical and emotional journey that the protagonist is going on. Who else is involved in your story and your hero's journey?

3. Is there an antagonist involved?

It's difficult to root for our protagonist if there's no challenge to overcome and challenge usually arrives in the form of an antagonist. The antagonist can take the form of a person, group of people or a situation. What's the barrier to your hero easily achieving their objective?

4. How did the protagonist venture into the unknown and overcome adversity and obstacles?

To achieve the objective and overcome the antagonist, our hero needs to take some risks. They need to be brave. They'll step outside of their comfort zone to confront all kinds of adversity and overcome large obstacles. How do they do this?

5. What valuable lesson was learnt?

To wrap up your story, there needs to be an obvious learning from the experience. The learning should, of course, link back to your initial objective for the story, driving through your message and getting stakeholders to buy in to your recommendations.

Putting this all together

Let's imagine you're trying to convince a product director to let you run a workshop, but they're resisting. Different stakeholders have competing priorities and you need alignment so the delivery team knows what to work on, but the product director is concerned that the workshop will just hold things up and create more friction. You decide to tell a story of a similar situation you've experienced, where you successfully persuaded a product director to run a workshop to get stakeholders aligned. Some of the key details for your story might include:

1. Who's the lead protagonist and how will your audience empathise with them?

Lily, a product director. She's under a lot of pressure to launch some new product features and is stressed out. She spends most of her time fending off stakeholders who are complaining that the product doesn't help them achieve their goals. She's worried about delays and doesn't want to waste time.

2. Who are the other characters?

Melissa, the CEO. Harry, the commercial director. Other stakeholders that Lily works with.

3. Is there an antagonist involved?

To some extent, the antagonist is Melissa, but mostly the antagonist is the situation: it's a high-value product and stakeholders can't agree on priorities.

4. How did the protagonist venture into the unknown and overcome adversity and obstacles?

Lily doesn't want to run the workshop. She thinks it will waste time and lead to more arguments. She steps into the unknown and lets the workshop go ahead, despite stakeholders being at each other's throats. She trusts me to run the workshop, which is difficult as there's so much at stake.

5. What valuable lesson was learnt?

When there's misalignment between stakeholders, get them together to decide on priorities. Don't bury your head in the sand and hope it'll all be OK. The product features launched behind schedule but only because we delayed running the workshop. If we'd have run the workshop earlier, we'd have launched on time.

It's your turn now

Think back to one of the objectives you've identified and a time when you achieved that objective. Take a few minutes to Record the key details for your story. You'll need all these so you can start to Apply an engaging structure.

Apply an engaging structure

In business storytelling, your story should ideally have four sections:

1. Segue

2. Set the scene

3. What happened?

4. Lessons learnt

1. Segue

Before you launch fully into your story, you'll need to introduce it to your audience. This isn't something you can fully prepare in advance; how you segue into the story depends on what's happening in the conversation. The key thing is to relate what's being said in the conversation to your story, explain why your story is relevant and pause to check everyone is OK with you telling a story. For example, if you want to tell the story about Lily the product director, you might say:

'You're obviously concerned about running this workshop. It's not part of the scope and you're worried it's going to lead to more friction and arguments. I've often been in this type of situation. In my previous role, we had a lot of pressure to launch by an impossible deadline, and like now, we wanted to run this workshop.'

Notice how the segue begins with empathy. You're demonstrating that you understand where the other person is coming from. When trying to influence someone's opinion, you should always lead with empathy and make it abundantly clear that you get their perspective.

Once you've shown empathy, you can start to introduce your story while continually relating it back to the current situation and what's at stake. Make it clear what the story's objective is and where you're heading with it. If your audience knows this, your story becomes more engaging. As your audience listens, their minds will keep trying to connect what you're saying with the conclusion you're heading towards.

Finally, you should pause for a brief moment after you segue to get tacit permission to tell your story. Occasionally, your story won't be welcome, so just in case, give your audience a second or two to tell you they don't want to hear it. Assuming they say nothing, you can launch full steam into your story where you'll start by setting the scene.

2. Set the scene

When setting the scene, make it clear whether you're telling a true or fictional story. You don't need to explicitly state which one it is – it just needs to be obvious when you set the scene.

Due to their authenticity, true stories are usually more persuasive than fictional ones. They're based on what actually happened so are instantly more believable (even though storytellers often embellish the facts). The best types of true stories are ones that you've been involved in. Often you won't be the protagonist, but if you witnessed the events first-hand then your story becomes more credible and more believable.

On the other hand, you can engineer a fictional story to fit your objective. This helps in crafting a compelling story, but when telling it you'll lack a bit of credibility. That said, a fictional story is usually better than no story. Remember those stats at the start of this chapter? Storytelling is almost always more engaging than regular conversation. For example, if you're introducing user journeys, designs and/or new features, it's often best to do so with storytelling. Presenting back what you did can quickly get boring for stakeholders.

Remember, most people that don't do your job are far less interested in the granular detail that enthrals you. Bring your work to life by telling a story of your protagonist, a fictional customer, accomplishing their goal with the new features.

When you set the scene, you'll also need to introduce the key characters and what they're trying to achieve. Start with your story's hero, the protagonist. Make them as relatable as possible by introducing them and their situation and highlighting the many similarities between what they're going through and what your audience is having to deal with. Your key aim is to quickly build lots of empathy towards your hero. Explain what's at stake so everyone immediately starts to root for the protagonist and worry what they might lose if they're unsuccessful on their quest. You'll also want to introduce your story's baddie, the antagonist. Remember, this might be a person, a group of people or even the situation your hero is confronted with.

There's a fine balance here between going into too much detail and not telling enough. You want there to be sufficient information for your audience to comprehend the situation, but not too much that you leave nothing to their imagination and they get bored. With practice, you'll get this balance right. Test out how you set the scene with team members and get their feedback. Continuing with our story about Lily the product director, here's how we might set the scene:

'The product director, Lily, is getting it in the neck from the CEO, Melissa, as the product hasn't launched yet. Lily's main goal for the product is to support customers. She's crazy-passionate about the customer experience. We also have the commercial director, Harry, and all he wants to do is upsell to customers. Lily is desperate for this product to go live as soon as possible and there's a lot riding on this for her.'

Or if you're presenting some new features, you might want to set the scene with your fictional protagonist:

'I'd like to introduce you to James, one of our typical customers. He needs help getting his new home ready for his young family to move in. There are only two weeks left until the big move and the new place is in a really bad state. He just wants things to be perfect for his family but is running out of time.'

In the second example, you'll go on to show how the new features will help James overcome his difficult experience. Let's look at how you might want to talk about what happened.

3. What happened

Now that you've set the scene, you can really get into the nitty-gritty of the story. Make sure you focus ruthlessly on the story objective throughout. Don't go off on tangents and don't provide side information if it doesn't link back to your ultimate objective. Again, test out your story with team members to get their feedback. You want your audience to stay focused and to listen the whole way through. Keep your story on track and your audience is far more likely to do this.

The two most important words to use when putting together the 'what happened' part, are 'therefore' and 'but'. You don't need to use these exact words when telling your story, but you should use them to keep you on track when you're planning how you'll tell your audience what happened. There needs to be action and a sense of things actually happening in your story. 'Therefore' implies forward momentum; you did something therefore something else happened. You'll also use 'and then', but be sure not to use it too many times without inserting 'therefore'. For example, 'I did this and then I did this, therefore this is what happened.'

'But' is the other connecting word you'll need when planning out how to relay what happened. 'But' introduces the obstacles: 'I did this and then I did this, therefore this happened but then this obstacle got in my way.' Crucially, 'but' creates tension – one of the most important feelings to evoke in your audience when telling stories. With 'but', you're building up doubt that the protagonist will actually achieve their objective. Your audience should be rooting for your protagonist, so will start feeling the tension running through their veins. Every time there's a 'but', try to demonstrate the grit and determination that the protagonist shows to overcome the obstacle. The harder it is and the more your protagonist pushes against adversity, the more the audience will root for them. By sprinkling in 'therefore' and 'but' throughout your story, you create a roller-coaster of emotions. Your audience should be on the edge of their seats.

Let's apply all this to our story about Lily, the product director. We've already segued into the story and set the scene, so now let's think about what happened:

> 'We tell Lily and her colleagues that we need to stop so we can realign on priorities.'

But…

> 'Lily refuses. She just needs this to go live as soon as possible. I don't know what to do as we want to support Lily as much as possible. Think about when you've been under that much pressure, you just can't see the wood through the trees.'

Therefore…

> 'We carry on.'

But…

> 'The requirements keep changing and a week later we're no further ahead. It's such a

nightmare, I don't know if I've ever been that stressed out, I'm barely sleeping at night.'

Therefore…

'I sit down with Lily again and she's totally broken too. Finally, she says, "OK, let's get this workshop booked in."'

Therefore…

'We have the workshop.'

But…

'The air is thick with tension. We're there with Lily and four of her colleagues.'

And then…

'We get into the detail, and we end up with two floor-to-ceiling columns of requirements. We're using all these green Post-it notes, so it's like a pair of beanstalks from *Jack and the Beanstalk*.'

But…

'Most of the requirements conflict with each other.'

And then…

> 'After three quite tetchy hours, and even with
> so many requirements, we manage to reach
> agreement on the priorities.'

4. Lessons learnt

Once you've segued into the story, set the scene and
then described the roller-coaster ride of what happened, you can wrap up your story with the lessons
learnt. This will often be the shortest of the four story
parts, and also the most important. If your audience
doesn't grasp the lessons learnt then there's no point
in you having told the story. The lessons learnt will
often be obvious. Assuming your segue makes it clear
where you're heading and you remain laser-focused
on the outcome when you describe what happened,
people will likely know the moral of the story.

You'll usually need just one to two sentences to wrap
up the story. Don't patronise your audience by spoon-
feeding them the conclusion, especially if it's obvious.
Let them have ownership of working out the moral
of the story and make the connection for themselves.
Wherever possible, you should use hard evidence (ie
data) to make your lessons learnt bulletproof and less
open to dispute. Sticking with our example of Lily, the
product director, I might use two sentences in the lessons learnt section:

'We were then able to launch four weeks later and we were only two weeks behind schedule. Had we done the workshop two weeks earlier, we'd have launched on time.'

Notice how I don't also say, 'Therefore it's always a good idea to run a workshop when stakeholders can't agree on priorities.' It's obvious and I'm granting power to the audience by letting them make the connection and owning that conclusion. By mentioning the number of weeks involved, I'm using data to add credibility to the conclusion.

Magnify engagement levels

Get the right structure of your story and you're halfway there. Make it really engaging, and you've got the other secret ingredient to using storytelling to influence, lead and build rapport.

Engaging vs boring your audience

All other things being equal, the more engagement techniques you use, the more likely it is that your story will persuade. At the same time, the more you use, the longer your story becomes and the more likely it is that people will switch off, so there's a balance to be had.

Generally speaking, you can tell longer stories (and use more engagement techniques) when you have everyone's attention for an extended period of time, when you're talking to Relators and Socialisers and when you become an experienced storyteller. You'll usually have everyone's attention for an extended period of time when you're delivering a presentation (you won't usually when you're in a meeting and lots of people are contributing), so embellish your story with a few of the engagement techniques outlined below.

Remember the different communication styles from Chapter 2? Relators and Socialisers tend to be more creative and are more likely to become engrossed in your story, so there's no need to hold back on the details with them. Directors and Thinkers tend to communicate in a structured and logical way and they'll likely want you to get to the point, so keep your story short for them and only use a few of the engagement techniques. Finally, your level of experience with storytelling will also dictate how many of the engagement techniques you use. If you're just starting out, go easy on yourself and don't use many (or even any) of these. Once you get accustomed to telling your stories, start bringing in a few of the engagement techniques and see how it goes.

There are a lot of techniques you can use to Magnify engagement levels. You wouldn't use all of them in one story as it'll be way too long. See which ones resonate the most with you and which you might want to try out. They fit into four categories:

- Get your audiences' minds working.

- Engage people's emotions.

- Use metaphors and similes.

- Bring your audience into the story.

Get your audiences' minds working

Our minds are always working in the background, trying to solve problems and fill in the gaps. When you overhear a conversation, you can quite easily zone it out and carry on with what you're doing, but what about when you overhear someone talking on the phone? It's distracting, hard to zone this out and feels really annoying. The reason for this is when you only hear half a conversation, it causes your mind to start working in the background, trying to fill in the gaps in the conversation.

You definitely don't want listening to your story to be as annoying as listening to someone talking on the phone, but you do want to get your audience's minds working in the background so everyone stays alert.

There are a few ways you can do this. First, intersperse your narrative with rhetorical questions. People's minds will actively start working to answer these questions. Questions should, of course, be related to the story, although there are a few questions which you could apply to almost any section of any story. For example, 'Do you know what I mean?', 'Can you imagine what that's like?' and, 'Do you know why?' can be used in many scenarios. When you're asking questions as part of your narrative, be sure to use the word 'you'. This makes it clear that you're aiming the question at your audience. Be sure to pause after you ask the question, just for a brief moment, to give people's minds a moment to start processing and answering the question.

As well as asking questions, you can repeat phrases and use repetitive language wherever possible. Doing so breeds familiarity for your audience and gets their minds connecting the words you're saying with the words you said a few moments ago. You can repeat one of your questions a few times. For example, you can ask the same generic question, 'Do you know what I mean?' or, 'You know why we did that?' a few times. You can also use repetition to describe how the protagonist is feeling during different parts of the story. You might say that, 'They were so stressed out…' and then a bunch of things happened, '…so they were still stressed out.' Then something else changed, and you know how they felt? You guessed it. 'They were still stressed out.'

Another way to use repetition is to use the same phrase in different parts of the story. Each time the big bad wolf tries to blow down the little pigs' houses, he starts by demanding, 'Little pig, little pig, let me in.' He invariably gets the response, 'Not by the hair of my chinny-chin-chin!' so replies by saying, 'I'll huff and I'll puff and I'll blow the house down.' This level of repetition makes the story more memorable. You may not want to talk about huffing and puffing in your workplace stories, but you can repeat phrases to show where you are on the journey towards the final objective. Things like 'it still didn't work', 'users kept complaining' and 'we still hadn't solved the problem' are all examples of phrases that you could repeat, depending on the story's context.

Finally, you should also keep relating the story back to challenges, people and situations that the audience is familiar with. Your segue will link the story to the current situation; that's its purpose. Be sure to do this in the rest of your story by using sentences that get your audiences' minds working, for example:

- 'Remember that time when (similar event) happened? This was just like that.'

- 'We were in a room just like the one we're in now.'

- 'She looks just like (famous person or someone your audience all know).'

Engage people's emotions

Once you've started to get people's minds working, you need to engage their emotions beyond the surface level. Share the protagonist's 'why' as soon as possible. Often, you'll do this when you set the scene, for example, 'She's crazy-passionate about customer experience.' Telling your audience what's happening accesses the neocortex part of their brains, the part responsible for rational thoughts. As soon as you move on to the 'why', your protagonist's purpose, you'll tap into the limbic system in the brain where feelings and decision-making happen. Storytelling is all about persuasion and influencing, so stimulating your audiences' limbic system is a really good thing. Nothing gets your audience to root for the hero more than understanding their 'why'.

Once your audience knows what's driving your protagonist, get them to imagine being there and feeling the same emotions. 'Imagine what this is like for them' and 'Imagine that you're there' are two really simple ways of doing this. If your audience knows what this is all really like for your protagonist, they can be by their side. Use strong emotions and adjectives in your storytelling to describe how people are feeling. Emotions such as surprised, shocked, scared and nervous are pretty strong; stick an adverb in front (eg very, extremely, totally, so) and they have even more impact. Statements such as 'Lily is crazy-passionate about customer experience', 'I don't know if I've ever been that stressed out' and 'she's totally broken' are all great examples of giving your audience real insight into what everyone is feeling throughout the journey.

Emotions can be joyous, although you'll usually reserve the happy feelings for the end of the story once our hero has completed their journey. Showing vulnerability will absolutely draw your audience in; boasting about achievements won't. Vulnerability can apply to everyone in the story: Lily's story shows her vulnerability as well as my own when I talk about being so stressed out that I'm barely sleeping at night. Displaying vulnerability is particularly effective for driving trust in you, your story and the outcome you're trying to achieve.

Use metaphors and similes

Metaphors and similes tap into people's subconscious, well beyond our analytical minds. They create images that the audience can instantly understand and which stay in their minds far longer than the words you use. You should definitely plan upfront metaphors or similes that you might use. To put them into your story, use this kind of sentence structure: 'She was so (insert emotion), she was like (insert metaphor / simile).'

Feel free to change any of the holding words; the main thing is that you say the emotion first and the metaphor or simile second. For example: 'He was so disappointed, he was like a giant beach ball deflating in front of us all,' or 'She was so surprised, she was like a rabbit caught in the headlights.' You can easily find metaphors and similes by searching for 'metaphors for (emotion)' online. Due to the way they get into our brains, metaphors are really powerful. When you haven't got time to tell a story or don't have a story to hand, you can fall back on using metaphors to engage and influence people.

Bring your audience into the story

The more you can get your audience to envisage themselves on the journey and by the side of your protagonist, the better. You can achieve this by being specific about some of the details. For starters, state the names of every character you mention in your story. Without names, people are anonymous and it's like you've never met them. Names are the unique identifiers for all the people in your story. Once we know everyone's names, we need to know a bit about them. For each person, what do they look like? How do they behave? What's their personality like? Who do they remind the audience of? Each time you describe a character, try to compare them to someone that the audience already knows (by appearance, behaviour and/or personality) – be it a famous person or some- one that you all work with. The more you describe the main characters, the more your audience is able to visualise and recognise them.

When you describe specific events where people are together, bring these to life with actual dialogue. By doing so, it's like your audience is overhearing an actual conversation. It gets them closer to feeling like they're really there, so is a powerful technique to Magnify engagement. Finally, tell your stories in the present tense. If you talk about an event that happened in the past, your audience can't feel they're in the room with you and the other characters. Talk in the here and now and they'll all be there with you, seeing what you see and sensing what you sense. That's Magnified engagement.

Accumulate your stories

In my experience, you only need a bank of five or so stories to support you in maybe 80% of the occasions where you might want to tell a story. When it comes to Defining the objective, it's amazing how frequently you'll have the same objective when trying to influence different stakeholders.

How do you Accumulate your stories over time? Simple. Any time you achieve an objective, you have a story. As soon as you get sign-off on a design, you secure additional engineering resources or you get an extension to a deadline, Record the key details, Apply an engaging structure to your script and then work out a few ways to Magnify engagement levels. Get into the habit of doing this any time you achieve success with anything. Before you know it, you'll have a lot more than five stories to choose from.

If you're really serious about getting some great stories, keep a diary while on the journey to achieving any objective. After any key event, write down the things that gave you (or someone else) a strong emotional reaction, for example, being surprised, shocked, scared or nervous. Try to get your whole team involved. It's far easier to do all this working in a group, so have a section in the agenda on storytelling as part of your regular get-togethers. What potential stories have you all collected? Who needs help in putting together a story? Who wants to practise telling a story?

Talking of practice, you should practise, practise, practise. As with stand-up comedians, you should do a dry run of all your stories with friendly team members. When getting feedback, ask questions such as:

- What objective did you think I was trying to achieve?

- Which parts did you find the most interesting?

- Where did you lose concentration?

- Which parts didn't add any value?

- What would you like me to do differently?

And so on. Many people find getting started with storytelling a bit overwhelming. There's a lot of information available on how to structure a story (eg the Hero's Journey). There's a lot less information on how to get going and starting with a blank sheet of paper is hard. Follow the DRAMA framework and hopefully you'll get to the second A in no time, where you're Accumulating lots of stories and able to roll them out as and when you need to influence, lead and build rapport.

In summary

To get going with storytelling, use this five-stage process:

- Define the objective

- Record the key details

- Apply an engaging structure

- Magnify engagement levels

- Accumulate your stories

So much of storytelling is about confidence. Having confidence that your story will be interesting. Having confidence that you can tell it well. Having confidence that you'll remember everything. Hopefully by following this framework, you can develop that confidence.

If you're filling in the self-retro, really think about how you currently tell stories and what you are and aren't doing. Regardless of where you think you're at, I urge you to get going with telling stories using the structure I've outlined:

❑ Get started with one story. The hardest part of storytelling is getting started, so get one story through the DRA part of DRAMA as soon as possible.

❑ Tell your story to one person. Practise your first story with someone that you trust and get their feedback.

❑ Pay attention to other people's stories. Storytelling happens all the time in meetings so listen to stories and analyse which engagement techniques people use.

A summary of the best practices in this book is available at www.humanpoweredbook.com/resources. Storytelling is the fifth component in this book's six-part model. Getting good at it can help you succeed at everything else in this book, so it's a great underlying skill to have. Our final chapter is all about outbound comms, of which storytelling often plays an important part.

SIX

Drive The Right Outcomes With Outbound Comms

What message are you conveying?

At work, you talk to colleagues face-to-face. You have meetings where you'll say things. You communicate over email and team chat. These are all examples of outbound comms, that is, times when you're trying to convey a message.

Some of the time you're in control of the topic (eg if you call a meeting or initiate the conversation) while at other times the other person is in control and you're responding.

Obviously in all these instances, you'll do active listening and seek a win-win outcome if there's even the tiniest disagreement (as per Chapter 1), you'll Adjust your communications style depending on what works best for the other person and not get triggered by how they communicate (Chapter 2), you'll use the LEAD techniques to influence them (Chapter 3), if you've called a meeting then you'll make sure everyone is Emotionally committed to being there (Chapter 4) and you'll get them all excited by telling stories that bring your data and facts to life (Chapter 5).

Assuming you're doing all of this now (wow, that's a lot!), the final thing is to finesse your outbound comms. All of your hard work can be undone if there's not enough clarity in everything you say and write down.

Whatever form your comms take – written or verbal, formal or informal, to one or to many – you should always have a clear objective and outcome you'd like to achieve. In Chapter 4, I told you not to bother book-ing in meetings if you don't know the outcome you want. In Chapter 5, I told you not to bother telling sto-ries if you don't know the outcome you want. In this chapter, I'm telling you not to bother communicating if you don't know the outcome you want.

You can easily define the outcome you'd like to achieve. Just complete this sentence: 'At the end of this communication, I want everyone to…' What you want could be almost anything. For example, you may want everyone to:

• Agree with your recommendations.

- Reach agreement on next steps.

- Contribute to resolving a particular challenge.

- Think that you're an expert.

- Strengthen their relationships with you and/or each other.

- Have fun.

- Laugh at your jokes.

And so on. You may want multiple outcomes from your outbound comms. Whether you're targeting one or many outcomes doesn't matter, as long as you're crystal clear on what you want to achieve.

You present a lot more than you may think

You're doing presentations way more than you might think, likely multiple times a day. The definition of a presentation is *not*: I have an accompanying slide deck when I speak. In fact, you need to get rid of (almost all of) those slides. More on slides in a bit. Let's get back to defining what a presentation is. According to the Oxford English Dictionary, it's 'A talk in which an idea is shown and explained to an audience'.

Basically, every time you tell someone something, show them what you're working on or explain something, you're presenting (even if it's just to an audience of one). If you're going to a meeting and expected to say something (beyond just asking questions), that means you're going to be presenting.

You need to prepare for every presentation you do, regardless of whether you're presenting for thirty seconds or for thirty minutes, or whether you're doing a formal presentation to senior stakeholders or briefly talking through something as part of an informal meeting. The amount of preparation you do will vary depending on how long you're likely to be talking for, who you're talking to, how well you know the topic and how important it is that you get the outcome you want.

Presenting and writing frameworks

Outbound comms covers two different mediums: presenting and writing. In both instances – and to stay in keeping with all the other chapters – there are specific frameworks for you to follow.

- Triple-S for presentation preparation: **S**tructure, **S**peech, **S**lides.

- Triple-R for presentation delivery: **R**oom, **R**oar, **R**espond.

- ABC for written comms: **A**void writing, **B**egin with the end in mind, **C**lear and concise.

Breaking down your outbound comms in this way allows you to be more strategic and more effective with what you're saying. You'll know the outcome you're trying to achieve and you'll be more likely to get it.

Triple-S for presentation preparation

Triple-S is generally a linear process when preparing for a presentation. Once you've finished creating the Structure, then you move on to creating your Speech, that is, what you're actually going to say. You should only get started on the next stage, creating your visual aids (your Slides) once you've worked out your Speech.

In my experience, most people do their presentation preparation backwards. Assuming a more formal presentation here, you create a slide deck, fill it with some images you like the look of, copy and paste some text to put your point across and away you go. Slides first, then you think about what you might say (Speech) and then finally you'll adjust the order of your key points to fit into some kind of Structure.

Doing it backwards isn't ideal, but the biggest mistake is doing no preparation, which, sadly, is far too common with minor, informal presentations or when you're expected to speak as part of a meeting.

Structure, Speech, Slides. That's the order and you should carry out *all* of these steps for whatever kind of presentation you're preparing for. Before I delve into the detail of the Triple-S process, let's take a look at the Rule of Three, something you'll need to know about when preparing for your presentation.

The Rule of Three

The Romans used to say *Omne trium perfectum* which, translated from Latin, means 'Everything that comes in threes is perfect'. When we talk about the alphabet, we say A, B, C. When we talk about numbers, we say one, two, three. Got different sizes? These are likely small, medium and large. Taking part in a competition? You're likely trying to win Bronze, Silver or Gold. There were three little pigs, three wise men and three musketeers. A genie always grants three wishes. You get the idea.

The Rule of Three has been around at least since the time of the Romans. More recently, a UCLA research study found that if you're trying to persuade someone then three arguments is optimal. Two isn't quite enough to persuade, but get carried away and add a fourth and it all starts to sound too good to be true. Once you know about the Rule of Three, you'll start seeing it all around you. Marketing messages, political speeches and news reports all use it extensively (notice my three examples here). Basically, most public outbound comms tap into the Rule of Three, so remember it when putting together and delivering your outbound comms.

OK, let's get going and put together this presentation.

Structure

When you create the Structure, start by defining the outcome you'd like to achieve. Remember, just complete this sentence: 'At the end of this presentation, I want everyone to…' I often get asked what's most important with presenting. Is it my body language? How confident I sound? How polished my slides look? These are all important, but in terms of delivering a successful presentation, nothing trumps knowing the outcome you'd like to achieve. If you don't have a laser-focus on your target outcome then nothing else matters. After all, how will you persuade anyone to do, think or feel anything if you don't even know what you want them to do, think or feel?

If someone asks you to do a presentation but you're not 100% sure why, then immediately ask them what the target outcome is. Defining your target outcome upfront will obviously increase the chances of you achieving it. Do this first, regardless of whether you're preparing for a thirty-second comment in a meeting or a thirty-minute formal presentation. If you're working on a presentation as part of a team, you should define the target outcome together and then physically surround yourself with it. Put the target outcome up on the wall if you're in a room together. Put it in every document and slide deck you use to help you plan and prepare. It's amazing how people get carried away and misalign what they're planning to say with the target outcome. All of you need to have that laser-focus on it.

Remember, a presentation doesn't mean you need to be standing up in a room in front of a bunch of people. Any time you're explaining an idea to someone else, you're presenting. You present a lot more than you think so you also need to define your target outcome a lot more than you think you do.

Hopefully you now understand the importance of always defining your target outcome first. What next? Now, it's time to break it down into three key messages to help you achieve the outcome. To do this, write a list of all the things you might need to say to achieve the outcome. This is ideation time so write down everything you can think of. It doesn't matter how long or short your list is.

Let's say you've got an upcoming meeting with an important stakeholder. The purpose is for you to update them on your work over the past six months and share your plans for the next six months. You obviously want them to be happy with the work your team has done, but that's not really your target outcome, it's a means to an end. Don't get these confused:

your target outcome is actually for them to sign off your proposed roadmap for the next six months.

You'll start by writing down all the things you might tell the stakeholder to hopefully achieve this:

- We ran three rounds of user research to explore our ideas.

- We had usability issues early on, but we've ironed them out.

- The team has put live feature A and here's how it works...

- The team has put live feature B and here's how it works...

- The team has put live feature C and here's how it works...

- We've already seen X% improvement in key metrics.

- Our roadmap aligns to the department's business priorities.

- We're confident the planned features can be built with our resource availability.

- We've tested initial concepts with users who have received them well.

OK, that's a long list and it's certainly more than three. Let's start putting items into a maximum of three groups and writing a one-line summary for each. Those will be our three key messages. We may end up with something like:

1. We've put live 90% of the features that we said we would six months ago.

2. Our research shows that users love the new features.

3. Our roadmap solves many problems for users and should lead to a vastly improved experience.

If you end up with more than three groups, then choose the most important three and get rid of the rest. Likewise, if you have items that don't fit into your top three groups, get rid of them. Less is often more and you should avoid diluting the most important messages with less important ones.

At this point, stop. Ask yourself, 'Who am I presenting to? What goals and concerns might they have? What's important to them?' Remember, your comms aren't for you, they're for the person you're presenting to, so if your key stakeholder is quite commercially minded, you might tweak these key messages as the last two focus on the customer experience. Perhaps your key messages become:

1. We've put live 90% of the features that we said we would six months ago.

2. Our research shows that users could easily do the things we wanted them to do.

3. Our roadmap solves many problems for users and should lead to conversion improvements and increased revenue.

Great, those key messages are looking good. You now need to work out what the key points are for each of your key messages. Again, follow the Rule of Three and list up to three key points for each key message. Based on the long list we came up with earlier, these might be:

1. We've put live 90% of the features that we said we would six months ago.

   a. Feature A is live and here's how it works…

   b. Feature B is live and here's how it works…

   c. Feature C is live and here's how it works…

2. Our research shows that customers are doing the things we want them to do.

   a. We ran three rounds of user research to explore our ideas.

   b. We had usability issues early on but we've ironed them out.

   c. We've already seen X% improvement in key metrics.

3. Our roadmap solves many problems for users and should lead to conversion improvements and increased revenue.

   a. Our roadmap aligns to the department's business priorities.

   b. We're confident the planned features can be built with our resource availability.

   c. We've tested initial concepts with users who have received them well.

Again, keep challenging yourself as to what goals and concerns your listeners have and adjust your key points. You've read Chapter 4 about facilitating meetings and taken it all onboard, right? Great. You should be an expert at preparing for meetings and proactively working out people's goals and concerns.

Phew, that's a lot of work. You haven't even thought about what you're going to say or even created a slide yet. Defining your Structure is the hard part, but once you crack it, everything is plain sailing. Your Structure forms the solid foundations for you to go on and create your Speech and then your Slides. Never leave out the Structure step. If you're preparing for a thirty-second comment in a meeting then this stage will hardly take any time at all and you'll likely have just one key message. If you're preparing for a thirty-minute formal presentation, you'll likely need all three key messages and some key points within them.

Speech

You've defined the Structure, the foundation of your presentation. Now you can start planning out what you're going to say for your key messages and each of their key points. Regardless of who you're presenting to, you'll almost always want to use the inverted pyramid style for your Speech. This means putting the conclusion first and following this up with the detail:

- Outcome
- Key message 1
  - Key point 1
  - Key point 2
  - Key point 3
- Key message 2

And so on. Journalists have been using the inverted pyramid style since the nineteenth century and most modern content producers use it today. People like hearing the conclusion first so they can understand where you're going with your Speech. If they know the conclusion upfront then they can connect your points with this as you go along.

As a general rule, you'll want to explain every point and then bring it to life with a story. The depth and focus of your explanation will depend on which type of person you're presenting to, as will the amount of time you spend storytelling. Having read Chapter 5 and hopefully put it into practice, you're now an accomplished storyteller with a bank of stories available. Also refer back to Chapter 2 and remind yourself of the four communication styles. If you're presenting to a small group and there's a key stakeholder in the room, decide which will work best for them. They'll primarily be interested in:

1. Achieving their own goals with little interest in how you get there (Directors).

2. The big picture and having game-changing impact (Socialisers).

3. Other people's opinions and whether these people are aligned to you (Relators).

4. Facts, data and the robustness of your process (Thinkers).

Let's look at each of these four styles in turn.

If your key stakeholder is a Director, keep it high-level and focus on how you're helping them achieve their goals. Talk about data and show plenty of evidence to back up everything you're saying. Tell stories to bring it all to life, but keep these brief.

For Socialisers, again, don't go into the detail, but this time focus on how what you're doing fits into the bigger picture. Go into a small amount of detail and then spend most of your time telling stories of what happened and what will likely happen so they get excited about the game-changing impact your work will create.

If you've got a Relator listening to your presentation, talk through what you've done slowly. As you go into the detail, focus on the people aspect and not the data. You'll need to demonstrate that what you've done fits with customers' and stakeholders' goals and ultimately makes them happy (you can bring this to life with storytelling).

Finally, for Thinkers – as with Relators – go into detail, but this time focus on facts and data. Do a bit of storytelling but keep it short. Talk through the process you've been through in depth and demonstrate the robustness of what you've done and how you used facts and data to make decisions.

Things get a bit less clear-cut if you're presenting to a few important stakeholders in the room who have a mix of communications styles between them. In these instances, you'll need to work out the right mix of detail, facts, personal opinion and storytelling. It's also tricky if your important stakeholder is a blend of two or three of these communications styles. If you really don't know the preferred style then you may just want to gamble on Director or Socialiser. Directors and Socialisers are more focused on the future and less interested in the detail, which generally tends to be the case with senior stakeholders.

Fortunately, you created your Structure first. The core presentation structure is designed to flex for any audience (another reason why starting with defining the Structure is so important). Within each key message and key point, simply change your explanation based on your key stakeholders' preferences while still getting your point across and achieving your target outcome. There's no need to write out your whole script in advance. Just decide on the main things you'll need to say to land each of those key messages and write them down. This is where you work out the right mix of detail, facts, personal opinion and storytelling. Once you've written all this down, come up with ways of personalising your messages so they feel really relevant to your key stakeholder. Drop in facts about them, their objectives, things they're working on, their team, etc. As I talked about in Chapter 3, you're more likely to Establish great rapport if they feel like you understand them. If you don't know much about them, do some online research, ask other people and/or ask them directly.

Next, work out all the opportunities for audience engagement and ideally, at least one per key message. Talking at people for more than a few minutes can get dull, so you should proactively plan for how you'll make your presentation interactive. This can be as simple as asking your audience, 'What do you think?' or 'What questions do you have?' a few times. You might ask them to raise their hands to a yes/no question or if you've got the time and it feels appropriate, get them to discuss something in pairs (using break-out rooms for virtual meetings) and then share their answers with the group.

There'll often be audience engagement after your presentation too, especially if you want everyone in the room to reach a decision. You'll need to use all the facilitation skills you learnt in Chapter 4 at this point to drive to your target outcome. Once you've worked out your engagement opportunities, write these down alongside your notes of what you're going to say against each key message.

Finally, think about the opening and closing statements. Your opening statement should never be, 'Thanks for coming to this meeting,' or anything even remotely as dull as that. You also shouldn't start with practicalities (timings, logistics, etc) or small talk (the weather, traffic, etc). Opening with, 'Hello,' and your name is equally dull, so if there's anyone that doesn't already know you, don't start by introducing yourself. Instead, your opening statement needs to immediately grab everyone's attention. You want people to look up and to be interested. You want them to feel surprised, shocked, scared or even nervous. A boring and uninspiring opening sets the tone for the rest of your presentation and you run the risk of fighting an uphill battle to get everyone's attention. An unpredictable and attention-grabbing opening tells your audience that they need to pay attention and they may miss out if they don't.

The first few words of your opening statement are perhaps the most important. They need to create intrigue so your audience are on the edge of their seats, wanting to know what comes next. The opening statement of your presentation might be:

> '"I would never buy this. How does anyone actually use this? I hate this."' (Dramatic pause.) 'Those are real quotes from customers using our previous system. "That was so easy! Is that all I need to do? I actually enjoyed that." Those are quotes from customers using our new features.'

Notice the Rule of Three with those quotes. If your key stakeholder is more focused on revenue, you might open with: 'One million pounds.' (Dramatic pause.) 'Since our new features have gone live, our product has generated an additional one million pounds in revenue.'

If you're not able to talk about revenue, you might reference other data: '30,000 people.' (Dramatic pause.) 'We estimate that 30,000 more people will use our product this year because of the changes we've made in the past six months. And we think this is just the start.'

Now you've grabbed everyone's attention, you can introduce yourself (if people don't know who you are), talk about logistics (although these are often best sent over before in a written message) and then segue into the main part of your Speech (ie your target outcome and key messages).

You'll often start your presentation a few minutes after the meeting has started to allow time for everyone to arrive and a bit of small talk. Delivering the opening statement is a great way to signal that the general conversation is over and you're now doing the presentation.

Once you've nailed down your opening statement, you'll need to create your closing statement. Most presentations end with 'Thank you', which is an appalling way to finish. Why are you thanking your audience? They should thank you for delivering such an inspiring presentation. Whatever you say at the end is going to stick with people, so while 'Thank you' is polite, it's hardly the key takeaway you want people to remember. What's the thing you most want your audience – and, in particular, the key stakeholder – to remember? Your target outcome. Your closing statement might be:

> 'We've achieved some really great results the
> past six months. Now we'd like your sign-
> off on our roadmap to keep the momentum
> going, so we can achieve even more in the next
> six months and help you to hit your revenue
> target.'

Putting all of this together, your Speech might look a bit like this:

- Opening Statement
- Intros / Logistics
- Outcome
- Key Message 1
  - Key Point 1
    - Facts / data
    - Story 1
    - Allaying concerns
    - People's opinions
    - Personalised message
    - Engagement opportunity
  - Key Point 2
    - …
- Closing Statement

I've included an example of all the different things you might want to cover in Key Point 1 but you're unlikely to include all of these in all the key points. What you include depends on the length of the presentation, who your audience is and so on. Remember, you're not writing down your entire script here. Instead, you're creating a plan for what you're going to say to land each of those key points and key messages and ultimately achieve your target objective. Now the bit you've been waiting for. You can crack on and make some Slides.

Slides

You've got your Structure in place, which you can flex regardless of who you're presenting to, the level of information you'd like to talk about and how long you have to present. Given these variables, you've worked out what you should be saying (your Speech). Now it's time to make your Slides.

Many people prepare for a presentation by creating a slide deck and thinking about what they'd like to visually show their audience. Not you though: you're not going to start that slide deck until you've defined your Structure and Speech, right? When you finally do get to work on your slide deck, you're going to keep telling yourself the number one rule of using slides: My slides will complement what I'm saying.

That's correct, the main purpose of your slides is to *complement* what you're saying. It is 100% not to *repeat* what you're saying. Look back over a slide deck you've used for a recent presentation. How much of it repeats what you said and how much of it complements? In my experience, remove the content that more or less repeats what you're saying and you get rid of maybe 80% of the slides. Then you can remove 80% of the words on the remaining slides.

Generally, slides are useful and if you're speaking for more than five minutes then you should absolutely use them (or other visual aids). They're great if you want to show something that's easier to explain visually than with words, such as designs and new features. They're also great for reminding the audience what you're talking about for those moments they switch off. I'm afraid your audience will switch off at times no matter how much you follow all these best practices and how amazing you are at storytelling. Remember, our minds wander during 47% of our waking hours so it's normal for people to switch off for a bit. Slides are also good for making your presentation memorable. Some people have visual minds, so showing images to support your points can help them recall what you've said later on.

Your slides are *not* there to remind you what you need to say or as a prompt for you. That's what notes are for. Sometimes you'll need to share your slides afterwards, in which case you'll need two versions: one that complements what you're saying during your presentation and another that's got all your key points written down so people can refer back to them later. In fact, you should generally aim for an absolute maximum of ten words per slide when presenting. Any more and people will be half-listening to you and half-reading the slides.

Hold on. You're really busy and you definitely don't have time to create *two* slide decks for every presentation. If you follow the Triple-S process, making a second slide deck as a handout is actually quite straightforward. Simply take your notes – basically all your key messages and key points – and copy and paste them into some blank slides. You may need to tidy them up a bit, but in reality, creating this additional slide deck should take minutes (and certainly not hours). If you're presenting a report then do the opposite. Remove almost all the words and only include visual aids that complement what you're saying. You can always copy and paste the words into the notes as a prompt for yourself.

Just to drive the point home: Don't put in reams of text that you read to the audience. Don't use bullet points in your slides when you're presenting (bullets are fine for handouts). Don't have more than ten words per slide. Your slides should augment and complement your words and not simply repeat them. Also be careful when presenting assets like designs or product roadmaps, which may have lots of words embedded in them. You may want to crop or blur out the parts you're not talking about or zoom in on the parts you are talking about to remove the distraction of too many words.

You've defined your Structure, worked out your Speech and created some Slides. Now you're ready to deliver your presentation. It's Triple-S to prepare, and Triple-R to deliver your presentation.

Triple-R for presentation delivery

Delivering your presentation is more than just speaking. You need to optimise the environment first (the physical or virtual Room) and once you start speaking (when you'll Roar), you'll likely need to answer questions and challenges (Respond) to help achieve your target outcome. I have a lot less to say about presentation delivery compared to preparing for your presentations. The most successful presentations aren't the ones where the presenter has a great delivery style (although this helps a lot). They're the ones where the presenter knows what outcome they want and has a Structure that supports achieving this. Keep reading to see how you can adjust how you deliver presentations, but don't forget that preparing properly is more important.

Let's dive into the Triple-R framework, starting with Room.

Room

While most people spend way too little time planning the Structure of their presentation, hardly anyone thinks about the Room. Big mistake. If you don't have the correct physical setup, whether you're presenting in person or remotely, it can derail the entire presentation.

Remember, your Slides are threadbare so your notes are your prompts and you'll need to make sure they're visible. You can usually have them open on your laptop while the screen shows your slides. Double-check this before your presentation and make sure you know how to set everything up and do any troubleshooting.

Some screens will simply reflect what's on your laptop so you may need to come up with a way around this (eg a second laptop just for your notes). If you aren't able to put your open laptop in front of you (eg if there's no table for it or if the cable doesn't stretch) you'll need to work out a solution such as bringing in a new table or getting a longer cable. In short, take the time to plan for the Room setup before your presentation. Get in there fifteen minutes before the start time and make sure everything is as you need it. A good trick is to invite your audience to join you fifteen minutes after you have access to the meeting room. If you're presenting offsite, then get a photo of the room and find out about the AV setup beforehand.

You'll usually want to be standing up when you present as you won't have the same energy level, gravitas or authority when sitting down. Make sure you can stand somewhere where you won't be blocking anyone's view of the big screen, where you can look at everyone in the audience throughout and, of course, where you can view your notes.

These principles generally apply when you're presenting remotely too (including standing up to present). Check everything beforehand and make sure you've got a way to look at your notes while presenting. Test out whatever software features you'll be using before-hand. Having two screens is helpful, just make sure your notes are somewhere near the webcam. Every-thing you don't check is something that can go wrong. One of the worst ways for you to start a presentation is to be messing around with the technology, trying to make it all work. You'll potentially get flustered and everyone will get bored waiting for you. First impressions are key so you want to get your impact-ful opening statement out there as soon as possible. Don't let technology or environmental challenges get in your way.

In Chapter 3, I talked about Looking for the basics and getting them right. Getting the Room working for you is a classic example of this. If you don't bother thinking about any of this, you may still get lucky and everything will be fine – but it may not. Why run the risk? I also talked about using people's names a lot in Chapter 3. A person's name is the sweetest sound in any language for that person, so if you don't know everyone's names beforehand, be sure to write these down in the order they're sitting.

Roar

So much has been written in books and online about how to be a better presenter. For me, the most impor-tant thing is that you go in excited and enthusiastic. As I talked about in Chapter 4, excitement is infectious, so if you're not excited, then you can't expect your audience to be. If you're excited about the outcome you're trying to achieve, your audience is far more likely to buy into it. That's why you should Roar when you deliver your presentation.

Even though you're Roaring, speak slowly and pause a lot. Your audience needs time to process what you're saying, so make it easy for them to do this. Top tips are to open your mouth wider than normal when speaking as this will naturally slow you down (sounds strange but it works) and write PAUSE in your notes between all of your key points and after you say something important. It's also easier for people to take on board what you're saying if you use informal, everyday language and short sentences. Address the audience as 'you' and your team as 'we'. Don't try and impress them with jargon and complexity. Talk directly to your audience, like you're having a conversation with them, albeit one where you're talking slowly, excitedly and with lots of pauses. Always look at your audience and never look at the screen. You'll automatically look at them if your notes are in front of you and in the same line of sight as them.

Finally, remember the LEAD techniques in Chapter 3. You can, and should, use many of these when presenting. These are all good influencing tactics and the reason you're presenting is to try to influence key stakeholders to agree to your target outcome. You should also lean heavily on the LEAD techniques when people interrupt you with questions and/or start challenging you, because how you Respond is as important as how you Roar.

Respond

You'll likely have to Respond during your presentation, when people interrupt you and once you've finished. Fortunately, having read most of this book you've got lots of tools to deal with even the toughest challenges. Generally, there are two types of questions that you'll face: Clarification Questions and Challenge Questions. Let's take a look at how to handle them.

Clarification Questions are really simple – you just respond with a short answer. If more than one of you is presenting, then make sure that only one of you answers. It gets boring quickly when each of you responds to the same question with a similar answer, but using slightly different words. Clarification Questions are simple questions where the other person doesn't fully understand what you're saying, so you can provide a simple answer followed by, 'Did I answer your question?' Don't forget to always end with a question. It's important that you invite the other person to keep the conversation going if they want to.

Most people tend to treat questions as Clarification Questions. The truth is, the vast majority are actually Challenge Questions. You'll get asked Challenge

Questions when someone in your audience doesn't fully agree with what you're saying and/or is concerned about something. They may not say, 'I don't agree,' or, 'I'm concerned,' though. Often, you'll need to pick this up in their tone of voice. If you're not sure whether you're being asked a Clarification or Challenge Question, err on the side of caution and assume it's the latter. Let's say you're facing a Challenge Question. The challenge basically represents the other person stating a problem that they have. What should you do if someone is stating a problem? Use the PLEASE process. They've explained the Problem for you, so you'll move straight into Listen and Explore before you Articulate your point of view and then Solve the problem together.

Imagine Andy is presenting to Zoe and she stops to ask him, 'How does this fit in with the roadmap that the other team is working towards?' It's a simple question which Andy is about to answer as he can easily clarify this. He stops himself though, as there's a certain tone in her voice. She sounds a bit concerned, so perhaps this is a Challenge Question? Having read this book, he decides not to respond and instead starts a PLEASE process. Zoe's question is the Problem, so he launches straight into actively listening.

Andy: 'OK, it sounds like you've got a few concerns with our plan and with it being misaligned with the other teams?'

Zoe: 'Yes, I do. You guys are too siloed from each other. Just because you're in a different team, it doesn't mean you can't work together. I'm seeing too much stuff going live without thought for the bigger picture. Our customers are starting to get a pretty inconsistent experience.'

Andy: 'That's really bad, none of us want that. You obviously launched our One Experience initiative last year. We all think it's a great idea and really want it to succeed. Can you tell me a bit more about the inconsistencies you're noticing?'

Zoe: 'There just seem to be different interactions and features across the different journeys. It's confusing for our customers.'

Andy: 'It is confusing, you're absolutely correct. I've checked with the leads in the other team and they seem OK with our plan. Do you think that's enough or should we check in with them once we flesh this out a bit more just to make sure there's a consistent experience when we start defining the detail?'

Zoe: 'I think you've answered your own question there.'

Andy: 'Yes, I guess I did. Not a problem. As an action from today, I'll set up those meetings and make sure we're regularly checking in with them. Is there anything else we can do to help with the One Experience initiative?'

Zoe: 'No, it's fine. I appreciate you doing that.'

Andy: 'Great, I'm really pleased we talked about that. Would you like to ask anything else, Zoe?'

Zoe: 'No, thanks.'

Andy could have answered her question straight-away by telling her he's already checked in with the other team. Instead, he took the time to explore where she was coming from so she feels listened to and validated and recognises that he's working to help her achieve her goal. The chances of him achieving his target outcome are greatly increased.

There is another instance where you'll want to lean on the PLEASE process when you're doing a presentation, although this time you'll be explaining the Problem. Let's assume you've organised the meeting, everyone attending has total clarity on the meeting objective and is Emotionally committed to being there (if not, please re-read Chapter 4). Even so, people can start having tangential conversations and you'll need to stop this happening if it goes on for too long. You'll be clear on the target outcome of your presentation, so if conversations are happening that aren't aligned to this then you have a problem. You'll want to say something like:

'Can I just interrupt you for a moment? Is that OK? Do you mind? Look, what you're discussing is a really important conversation to have. I'm just aware of the time and obviously the objective of this meeting is to agree on the future roadmap. What do you want to do?'

You're using the 'But you are free' technique from Chapter 3 here, to hopefully get the discussion back on track.

ABC for written comms

It's hardly surprising that, when given a choice, 80% of people prefer clear English (according to research by a Michigan Law School).[27] What is interesting though, is that the more educated the person and the more specialised their knowledge (which may or may not tie in with seniority), the greater their preference for plain English is.

As with delivering your presentation, a huge amount has been published about how to write well. In my experience, most people don't enjoy learning about written comms as they feel they already know it all (and they probably do). What people say they know and what they actually do in reality can be different and people's written skills are generally below par, so there's a short section in this book dedicated to written comms. While it doesn't contradict general best practices for written comms, the ABC framework does have a slightly different slant on things.

Avoid writing

The most important thing you can do when it comes to written comms best practice is to stop writing as much as possible. Pick up the phone, jump on a video call or speak directly to the other person. Stop defaulting to written comms – it may seem quicker and easier but it can lead to longer conversations and misunderstandings.

It's all too easy to quickly write things down, and it's even easier for the other person to misinterpret what you mean. With written comms you're limited to your words – body language and tone of voice don't come into it. Albert Mehrabian's (oft-quoted) research found that what you say only accounts for 7% of the impact when you're talking about feelings and attitudes. Tone of voice and body language account for 38% and 55% respectively, so when you use written comms, you're losing up to 93% of the impact.[28] Without tone of voice or body language, what you're trying to say can easily be misinterpreted. Even if you don't take these into account, we all have different upbringings, different experiences and come from different backgrounds. All of this makes it so easy to interpret things differently. What you say and what the other person thinks you mean can be two different things. Have a verbal conversation and, as well as picking up on tone of voice or body language, it's easy to ask Clarification Questions on the fly. The conversation ebbs and flows so there's a greater chance of everyone understanding.

What you don't say in written comms can have as much of a negative impact as what you do say. The reassurances that you don't provide and the concerns you don't respond to can fester for the other person. In verbal comms, you can usually pick up on these and help the other person to resolve these. You might be inadvertently communicating in a negative way in your written comms and you won't know if you can't see the other person's reaction. Go back to Chapter 2 and remind yourself of any negative behaviours you might be displaying.

Finally, whatever you write down remains there in perpetuity. The way you feel when you write something may not be how you feel later on (especially if your emotions were raised at the time of writing). The opinions you put across when writing may not be the opinions you have later on. The spelling and grammar mistakes you included can't usually be changed. In short, written comms are there forever and you may not want them to be.

There are some notable exceptions to Avoiding writing. Quick and/or functional comms are fine to be handled through team chat, for example, things like setting up an informal meeting, asking a quick question, sharing a useful article and so on. Most of your day-to-day comms are functional, so there's nothing wrong with sending quick messages over team chat. In fact, messages sent on team chat often work well as they allow the recipients to respond when they're available. If the written conversation evolves and moves away from being functional though, immediately end it and have a verbal conversation.

On the opposite spectrum, complex explanations (technical specifications, reports, etc) should, of course, be written up into a document. Also and as I explained in Chapter 2, when you're introducing a Problem as part of the PLEASE conflict resolution process, it's often good to tee this up over email or team chat. This gives the other person time to get their head around the issue and prepare for the face-to-face conversation. Remember Chapter 4 on facilitation? When you're running a meeting, your pre-meeting comms and action list are also best delivered written down.

It's easy to write, but it's usually better to talk. Having read almost all of this book (yes, you're nearly finished), you're now armed with new skills that will hopefully give you confidence to have more face-to-face conversations in person or over video. Apart from the above exceptions, please Avoid writing as much as possible.

Begin with the end in mind

If you are writing, be sure to know your outcome. Knowing your target outcome has been mentioned a lot in this chapter – and indeed throughout the book – and written comms are no exception. Whether you're writing an in-depth report or having a quick conversation on team chat, make sure you know what you're trying to achieve. Remember, just finish this sentence: 'At the end of this communication, I want everyone to...' Begin your written comms with the target outcome (as with verbal comms and presentations) and then use the inverted pyramid style to form your structure: conclusion first, followed by the detail.

Clear and concise

A biography of Woodrow Wilson, who served as US President in the early 1900s, claims that he was once asked how long he spends preparing for speeches:

> 'That depends on the length of the speech. If it's a ten-minute speech it takes me two weeks to prepare. If it is a half-hour speech it takes me a week. If I can talk as long as I want to it requires no preparation at all. I am ready now.'[29]

Being Clear and concise is where most people struggle when it comes to written comms. One of the most important things you can do is to write conversationally, as if you're actually saying it aloud to someone else. Read through what you've written and ask your-self, 'Would I really say this?' If the answer is no, then you'll need to make changes.

Be ruthless with your text. If any part of what you're writing isn't 100% crucial then remove it. If you're not sure, take it out and then re-read what you've written. Has the meaning of what you're saying been changed by removing the text? If not, keep it out. For longer documents, break up your text with headings and bul-leted lists to make it more scannable. Keep sentences short (maximum ten to fifteen words per sentence as a general rule of thumb) and no more than five lines or so per paragraph. (Many of the paragraphs and sentences in this book are longer than I'd ever use at work. Unless you're writing a book that's supposed to be read in-depth, make sure your written comms are easy to scan.)

Finally, get the basics right: remove jargon and acro-nyms that your audience won't understand, spell everyone's name correctly (getting this wrong is a cardinal sin) and do a spelling and grammar check before you send anything.

In summary

When it comes to presentation preparation, it's: Structure, Speech, Slides.

When delivering your presentation, it's: **R**oom, **R**oar, **R**espond.

When you're using written comms, remember: **A**void writing, **B**egin with the end in mind, be **C**lear and concise.

There's lots for you to get on with in this chapter, especially if you have an upcoming presentation. Write up where you're at in your self-retro and then I suggest you start with these three initial actions:

- ☐ Always define your outcome. Whatever and however you're communicating, make sure you know the outcome you're trying to achieve.

- ☐ Remember the Rule of Three. Generally, create three arguments for every point you try to get across.

- ☐ Stop writing so much. With the new skills you've gained from this book, you'll hopefully have more confidence to speak with people.

Outbound comms is the final part in this book's six-part model. You'll use everything you've learnt in this book in your comms and everything in this chapter to bring clarity into what you say and write down.

Putting It All Together

You'll succeed with people skills

Toby and Ros work in different businesses and they both have a big meeting tomorrow.

Toby is presenting his team's work to key stakeholders and hoping to get agreement on next steps. He sent out the invite weeks ago, so hopefully they'll all turn up on time and not get side-tracked like they usually do. His team has achieved a lot, so he's got a whole bunch of slides to get through. His main objective is for everyone to understand what his team has done and just how hard they've worked. It's important they know this. When he finishes his presentation (assuming they let him get to the end), he'll work out what the next steps should be and tell them what his team could be doing next. These meetings can get a bit heated, but he's pumped up and ready to fight for what he believes to be right.

Ros is also presenting her team's work and hoping to get sign-off on her plan for next steps. She's clear on her target outcome for the meeting and has pro-actively tried to allay stakeholders' concerns in the run-up. She's reached out to them all a few times so they should all know why they're there and remain focused. Her most important stakeholder uses the Socialiser communication style, so she's planning to explain the big impact her team wants to have and to tell stories that bring their work to life. She's not plan-ning to get into the nitty-gritty of what they've been doing. There are some big decisions that need to be made and she's planning to use the 'But you are free' technique to encourage stakeholders to sign off what she'd like to do. She's also been practising PLEASE, so is ready to actively Listen in response to any concerns or Challenge Questions that get thrown at her.

All other things being equal, Ros is far more likely to succeed in her meeting and get the outcome she wants. Your hard skills go a long way to helping you get your job in the first place, but it's your people skills that help you succeed in your role.

Rome wasn't built in a day

It's not easy to do everything I recommend and it's even harder to make it habitual. If all this was simple, then everyone would be doing it and you wouldn't even need this book. Ros might have read this book, but she's also continually referred back to it over time to help her put everything into practice.

Depending on what stage you're at in your personal development, it's likely to take you months, or even years, to master the skills across the six topics I've outlined in depth:

1. Conflict resolution

2. Strong relationships

3. Leading and influencing

4. Facilitation

5. Storytelling

6. Outbound comms

It's doable though. You'll need to go through the four stages of learning: Unconscious Incompetence, Conscious Incompetence, Conscious Competence, and finally, Unconscious Competence.

You may not have heard of, thought about or put into practice some of the best practices I've outlined. In these instances, you're at learning stage one, which is when you have Unconscious Incompetence.

By reading this book and taking on board some of the recommendations, you'll find yourself at stage two, Conscious Incompetence. You've learnt some new things, but without practice, you won't be good at them. Awareness is a great start, though.

The biggest leap is to get to the next stage. Whereas moving from stage one to two is all about awareness, moving from stage two to three is about action. The more you practise your new skill, the better you'll get. Do this repeatedly and eventually you'll get to Conscious Competence. You're aware of what you're doing and you're getting quite good at it.

Keep going, and eventually you won't need to try anymore. You'll reach stage four, Unconscious Competence, when the skill becomes second nature. You're doing it, but you won't really be aware, as it's become habitual.

Reading this book is the easiest part. The hard work begins now. What are you going to do next? Will you put down this book and carry on with your job day-to-day or will you create an action plan and continually refer back to the best practice guidance so you do things differently? I really hope you choose the latter as the rewards can be great.

Do everything in this book and you'll get noticed more at work. You'll increase the chances of succeeding in your role, of attaining that promotion and of getting a pay rise. The skills you develop from reading this book can bring much more, though. Life is more rewarding when you know how to get on with people, how to lead and inspire them and how to help them be high-performing. This doesn't only apply to work; it applies to all aspects of life. Pretty much everything in this book also applies to your personal life and how you relate to your friends and family.

In short, I urge you to use this book as a reference guide on an ongoing basis. You'll learn a lot about yourself and you'll notice positive change in all your relationships. Don't forget to download our handy self-retro template and use the Framework Cheat Sheet below to keep you focused on the methods. A downloadable version of the Cheat Sheet, and the self-retro, are available at www.humanpoweredbook. com/resources.

Framework cheat sheet

Conflict resolution	Strong relationships
Problem is explained	**M**ap out people's communication styles
Listen and validate the other person's viewpoint	**A**djust your communication style accordingly
Explore in depth what success looks like for the other person	**S**uppress your negative behaviour
Articulate what success looks like for you	**T**ake ownership of difficult situations
Solve the problem by brainstorming a win-win outcome	**E**mpathise and assume the best of intentions
Enjoy the success and celebrate together	**R**eframe for strength and resilience

Leading and influencing	Facilitation
Look for the basics and get these right	**R**esponsibility for the meeting success is with you
Establish great rapport	**E**motional commitment – get everyone choosing to attend
Amplify your impact	**A**ssertively lead the room
Delight stakeholders continuously	**D**rive everyone to the outcome
	You are accountable for all action items

Storytelling	Outbound comms
Define the objective	Presentations:
Record the key details	**S**tructure, **S**peech, **S**lides
Apply an engaging structure	**R**oom, **R**oar, **R**espond
Magnify engagement levels	Written comms: **A**void
Accumulate your stories	writing, **B**egin with the end in mind, **C**lear and concise

Getting good at all this

The aim here is to achieve Unconscious Competence, but this book is jam-packed with best practices, so where do you even start? If you've created a self-retro as you've been working through the book, you'll now have a long list of 'What I do well' and 'What I can do better'. If you haven't, now's a great time to do this. Show your list to a few trusted peers to get their feedback. Other people may disagree with your reflections on what you're doing well and what you can do better, so it's well worth doing this.

Then, create a third section in your self-retro entitled, 'What I'm working on'. Move three items from the 'What I can do better' column into this new section and then consciously begin to practise these. When you feel like you're getting competent with an item, move it over to the 'What I do well' section and then place another item in the 'What I'm working on' section. In short, you want to always be working on three skills at a time – enough to keep you busy but not too much that you're overwhelmed. As well as practising your new skills, keep an eye on what other people do in terms of good and bad practice. Notice how some people engage stakeholders really well and how others exhibit negative behaviour that creates challenging situations. Try and work out what's going on and which best practices they're adhering to (or not).

In terms of what you prioritise, that's up to you. Think about your upcoming meetings or something that's been bothering you for a while. What do you feel empowered to now go on and solve? You may wish to prioritise simply based on the sequence in this book, as the six core topics do build on each other (conflict resolution and PLEASE underpin the other five topics). Ultimately though, you should prioritise what you think is likely to have the most impact. All the best practices in this book are guidelines and some of them may not work for you. That's OK. You need to find your own way so don't feel like you have to follow what this book says to the letter.

If everyone you work with exhibits the skills in this book, work gets better for everyone and your team, department and/or business is likely to thrive. Transformational change takes a lot of time and a huge effort and I urge you to play your part in this. Gandhi is often credited as saying that, 'You must be the change you want to see in the world.'[30] Regardless of how your colleagues behave, stay true to the core skills and ethos of this book. Your behaviour will impact other people, and over time, people will start to develop some of your skills simply by unconsciously mirroring what you do.

Driving large-scale change

If you're in a position of leadership and would like your team to exhibit the skills, behaviours and attitudes outlined in this book, then this is absolutely possible. To start, do a self-retro and apply it to your team as a whole. For all the best practices in this book, make a note of 'What we generally do well' and 'What we can generally do better'. Note the word 'generally' here – you'll obviously have a wide range of skills across the team, so you'll need to use gut feel to assess where you think your team is at on average.

Remember the Mere Exposure Effect from Chapter 3? People will get familiar with a message when they're exposed to it ten to twenty times, so only telling your team once which skills you'd like them to work on is unlikely to have much of an effect. Bringing about large-scale change takes a lot of time, sustained effort and repeated communication. Once you've got your long list of skills, start to prioritise. Which improvements are likely to have the biggest impact for the least amount of effort? Apply the Rule of Three here and choose your top three to focus on, ideally for a period of a month or so. You can then move down the list to your next three, and so on.

There's one key thing you can do to successfully drive through behaviour change, and that's to make sure that the conversation keeps going. For each new skill or behaviour, aim for everyone to be involved in a discussion about it ten to twenty times. This won't happen by chance. It will need to be intentional and you'll need to add it to the agenda of as many recurring meetings as possible.

Talk about the skills in your all-hands meetings. You'll need to explain which three skills you'd like everyone to focus on for that month, and why. Get people to have conversations in small groups about how they might use these skills. Don't dictate what they should do. Instead, tell them the behaviours you'd like them to exhibit and have them work out how they might do this. Once you've introduced the skills you'd like people to work on, have a specific agenda item about them in every all-hands meeting. As a leader, you should share successes and failures of how you've practised your new skills. You can also get people to practise in role plays, share what they've done in small groups and/or nominate people they've seen successfully using the new skills.

Keep the conversation going on team chat too. Again, lead by example and share your successes and failures, and encourage other people to do so as well. Put the skills into everyone's development plans and have line managers discuss these with people in their one-to-ones. You could even add an item to the agenda in all your daily stand-ups. Have the team ask themselves how they could use these skills to help with what they're working on. Which skills might help them to progress what they're doing?

Finally, you'll need to document the new skills and behaviours that you'd like people to be exhibiting. Adding these to process documents, behavioural frameworks and values are all good things to do.

When you're bringing in new people to your team, make sure these skills and behaviours are assessed during the selection process and then written down in the induction pack.

As with anything, the more you put in and the more you lead by example, the more everyone gains. As I said in the Introduction, there's a better way of you all working together and it will make everyone happier and increase your impact in the business. Behavioural change doesn't happen overnight. It takes a lot of time, effort and head space. If you're in a position of leadership, you might feel that these are all in short supply, but if you are able to do this, the rewards are there for the taking. Hopefully after reading this book, you'll agree that it's well within your grasp.

Notes

1. National Soft Skills Association, 'The Soft Skills Disconnect' (National Soft Skills Association, February 2015) www.nationalsoftskills.org/the-soft-skills-disconnect, accessed 10 May 2021
2. Hokkaido University, 'Nodding Raises Likability and Approachability' (MedicalXpress, November 2017), https://medicalxpress.com/news/2017-11-likability-approachability.html, accessed 10 May 2021
3. Dr T Alessandra, *The Platinum Rule: Discover the four basic business personalities and how they can lead you to success* (Warner Books, Inc, Sept 2014)
4. S Hanke, 'Three Steps to Overcoming Resistance' (*Forbes*, Aug 2018), www.forbes.com/sites/forbescoachescouncil/2018/08/14/three-steps-

to-overcoming-resistance/?sh=24594b665eae, accessed 10 May 2021

5. Matriarchies of Today & The Past, *The Bemba, Zambian Northeast Plateau* (Matriarchies of Today & The Past, no date), http://mmstudies.com/matriarchies/bemba, accessed 13 May 2021

6. C Porath and C Pearson, 'How Toxic Colleagues Corrode Performance' (*Harvard Business Review*, no date), https://dk4m.files.wordpress.com/2010/10/toxic-colleagues1.pdf, accessed 10 May 2021

7. M Hancock and N Zahawi, *Masters of Nothing: How the crash will happen again unless we understand human nature* (Biteback Publishing, 2011)

8. A Chamberlain, 'Does Company Culture Pay Off? Analyzing Stock Performance of "Best Places to Work" Companies' (Glassdoor, 2015), www.glassdoor.com/research/app/uploads/sites/2/2015/05/GD_Report_1.pdf, accessed 30 May 2021

9. R Karlgaard, 'Combat Consultant: Q and A with retired General Stanley McChrystal' (*Forbes*, 3 October 2017), www.forbes.com/sites/richkarlgaard/2017/10/03/combat-consultant-qa-with-retired-general-stanley-mcchrystal/?sh=480c02012f44, accessed 3 May 2021

10. Sigl, 'Marketing Fundamentals: The rule of 7' (Sigl, no date) https://siglcreative.com/2019/06/07/rule-of-7, accessed 10 May 2021

11. A Luttrell, 'The Mere Exposure Effect' (Social Psych Online, March 2016), http://socialpsychonline.com/2016/03/the-mere-exposure-effect, accessed 10 May 2021

12. *Harvard Business Review*, 'A Face-to-Face Request is 34 Times More Successful Than an Email' (APS, April 2017), www.psychologicalscience.org/news/a-face-to-face-request-is-34-times-more-successful-than-an-email.html, accessed 10 May 2021

13. A Lavole, 'Study: Know thyself and you'll know others better' (*The Harvard Gazette*, 20 March 2008), https://news.harvard.edu/gazette/story/2008/03/study-know-thyself-and-youll-know-others-better, accessed 10 May 2021

14. Convertize, 'Ben Franklin Effect Definition' (Convertize, no date), https://tactics.convertize.com/definitions/ben-franklin-effect, accessed 13 May 2021

15. K Hedges, 'The Do-Over: How to correct a bad first impression' (*Forbes*, Feb 2015), www.forbes.com/sites/work-in-progress/2015/02/10/the-do-over-how-to-correct-a-bad-first-impression/?sh=6c98092355f6, accessed 13 May 2021

16. RB Cialdini et al, 'Reciprocal Concessions Procedure for Inducing Compliance – The Door-in-The-Face Technique', *Journal of Personality and Social Psychology 31*(2), 206–215. https://doi.apa.org/doiLanding?doi=10.1037%2Fh0076284, accessed 13 May 2021

17 C Carpenter, 'A Meta-Analysis of the Effectiveness
    of the "But You Are Free" Compliance-Gaining
    Technique', Communication Studies 64:1, 2013,
    www.tandfonline.com/doi/full/10.1080/1051097
    4.2012.727941, accessed 13 May 2021

18. D Carnegie, *How to Win Friends and Influence
    People* (Vermilion; new edition, April 2006)

19. DJ Leach et al, 'Perceived Meeting Effectiveness:
    The role of design characteristics', *Journal of
    Business and Psychology* 24(1): 65–76, www.
    researchgate.net/publication/227024372_
    Perceived_Meeting_Effectiveness_The_Role_of_
    Design_Characteristics, accessed 13 May 2021

20. Atlassian, 'You Waste a Lot of Time at Work'
    (Atlassian, no date), www.atlassian.com/time-
    wasting-at-work-infographic, accessed 13 May 2021

21. GN Tonietto et al, 'When An Hour Feels Shorter:
    Future boundary tasks alter consumption by
    contracting time', *Journal of Consumer Research*
    45(5) 2019: 1085–1102, https://academic.oup.
    com/jcr/article-abstract/45/5/1085/4996321,
    accessed 13 May 2021

22. L Perlow, et al, 'Stop The Meeting Madness:
    How to free up time for meaningful
    work' (*Harvard Business Review*, July-August
    2017), https://hbr.org/2017/07/stop-the-
    meeting-madness , accessed 13 May 2021

23. MA Killingsworth and DT Gilbert, 'A Wandering
    Mind Is an Unhappy Mind' (*Science*, November
    2010), https://wjh-www.harvard.edu/~dtg/

KILLINGSWORTH%20&%20GILBERT%20 (2010).pdf, accessed 13 May 2021

24. K Hedges, 'How To Tell A Good Story' (*Forbes*, December 2013), www.forbes.com/sites/work-in-progress/2013/12/11/how-to-tell-a-good-story/?sh=3634aba9584c, accessed 13 May 2021

25. K Harrison, 'A Good Presentation Is About Data And Story' (*Forbes*, January 2015), www.forbes.com/sites/kateharrison/2015/01/20/a-good-presentation-is-about-data-and-story/?sh=139834bd450f, accessed 13 May 2021

26. J Campbell, *The Hero With A Thousand Faces: The Collected Works of Joseph Campbell* (New World Library; 3rd edition, 2012)

27. GDS team, 'Guest Post: Clarity is king – the evidence that reveals the desperate need to re-think the way we write' (Gov.UK, February 2014), https://gds.blog.gov.uk/2014/02/17/guest-post-clarity-is-king-the-evidence-that-reveals-the-desperate-need-to-re-think-the-way-we-write, accessed 13 May 2021

28. N Belludi, 'Albert Mehrabian's 7-38-55 Rule of Personal Communication' (RightAttitudes.com, October 2008), www.rightattitudes.com/2008/10/04/7-38-55-rule-personal-communication, accessed 13 May 2021

29. J O'Byrne, 'Writing a Long Speech Took Wilson No Time at All' (*Financial Times*, August 2018), www.ft.com/content/3b8fb324-9bf5-11e8-9702-5946bae86e6d, accessed 30 May 2021

30. The Publications Division, Ministry of
    Information and Broadcasting, Government of
    India, *The Collected Works of Mahatma Gandhi*
    (Volume XII, April 1913 to December 1914),
    www.gandhiheritageportal.org/

Online Resources

Want to keep going with your learning? Sign up to our five-part email skills programme and get a different lesson in your Inbox every week for five weeks at www.humanpoweredbook.com/email-skills. You can find our other resources at:

1. Communications style quiz – www. humanpoweredbook.com/comms-quiz

2. Framework cheat sheet – www. humanpoweredbook.com/resources

3. Self-retro template – www.humanpoweredbook. com/resources

4. Summary of best practices – www. humanpoweredbook.com/resources

Acknowledgements

I interviewed more than fifty digital, product, technology and design leaders to provide expert guidance for this book. Thank you for giving up the time to speak with me (job titles correct at time of interview):

Alice Newton-Rex, Chief Product Officer at WorldRemit

Amanda Neylon, Director of Insight, Data and Technology at Versus Arthritis

Andrew Merryweather, Vice President of User Experience at Elsevier

Ash Clay, Head of User Experience

Ash Roots, MD of Digital at BT

Bede McCarthy, Head of Product at Channel 4

Chris Thorn, Deputy Digital Delivery Director at Department for Work and Pensions

Danny Gonzalez, Chief Digital and Innovation Officer at London North Eastern Railway

Darci Dutcher, Senior Director, Product Design and Research at Typeform

Dave Priestley, Chief Digital Officer at Vitality

Dave Wascha, Chief Product and Technology Officer at Zoopla

Diarmaid Crean, Chief Digital and Technology Officer at Sussex Community NHS Foundation Trust

Emma Stace, Chief Digital and Technology Officer at Department for Education

Gavin Edwards, Global Head of Product Design and Research at London Stock Exchange Group

Giles Offen, Chief Digital Information Officer at Just Group

Guy Magrath, Director at GHM Digital

Helen Mott, Head of Digital at Ministry of Justice

Ian Morgan, Chief Digital Officer at Huber Holdings and PD Courtaulds Group

James Godfrey, Head of Digital Product & Experience at TUI Group

James Peddar, Chief Digital Officer at Domestic & General

Jane Austin, Chief Design Officer at Flo Health

Jo Wickremasinghe, VP of Product at Zoopla

Jono Hey, Chief Product Officer at Zen Educate and creator of Sketchplanations

Jora Gill, Chief Digital Officer at SHL

Julie Dodd, Director of Transformation at Parkinson's UK

Lara Burns, Chief Digital Officer at The Scouts Association

Martin Dowson, Head of DesignOps and EcoSystems at Lloyds Banking Group

Matthew Timms, Chief Digital and Technology Officer at E.ON

Michael Spiteri, Global Head of Transformation & Innovation at HSBC

Neil Roberts, Chief Product Officer at Papier

Nick Flood, Managing Director, Digital at Dennis

Noel Lyons, Chief Design Officer at Barclays

Paola Miani, Head of Design Culture at Lloyds Banking Group

Patrick Wyatt, VP Product at Deliveroo

Phil Jordan, Group CIO at Sainsbury's

Phil Young, Chief Technology Officer at Virgin Red

Phillip Julian, Head of Client Experience Design and Digital Strategy at Schroders

Rahul Welde, EVP Digital Transformation at Unilever

Regan Andrew, Consultant & Owner at Kearada.com

Richard Beaumont, Design Chapter Area Lead at Direct Line

Rob Muir, Chief Digital Officer at National Express

Robert Fransgaard, VP Experience Design at Sage

Robert Newham, Director of Design at Legal & General

Russ Thornton, Chief Technology Officer at Shawbrook Bank

Sandra González, Founder and Director at UX for Change

Scott Chow, Chief Product Officer at Beamery

Sean Gilchrist, Chief Digital Officer at Co-operative Bank plc

Stephen Scott, Chief Digital Officer at IAG Loyalty

Steve 'Buzz' Pearce, SVP Design at Checkout.com

Storm Fagan, Chief Product Officer at JUST EAT

Tim Buchanan, Digital and Marketing Director at Hiscox

Tom Read, CEO & Director General at Government Digital Service

Vanessa Kirby, Former Head of Experience Design at Argos and Marks & Spencer.

An even bigger thank you goes to Andrew, Ash, Bede, Chris, Jono, Neil and Alex Baxevanis (Head of Experience Design at Reason) for reviewing the manuscripts and working tirelessly to help shape this book. Thank you so much; your input was invaluable.

The Author

Trenton Moss is a business leader, trainer and coach who inspires those around him to achieve more than they think they can. He's a qualified leadership coach, a former Samaritan (where he provided face-to-face and telephone counselling) and he's been coaching and training teams for twenty years.

Trenton is founder and head coach at Team Sterka, a training and coaching business that creates high-performing digital product teams. He conceived and set up the People Skills as a Service programme, which transforms people's behaviour and gives them lifelong skills in leadership, emotional intelligence, resilience and a lot more.

Previously, Trenton set up, scaled and then (after a successful acquisition) exited one of the UK's leading experience design agencies. During his fifteen-year tenure as CEO of Webcredible, he trained, coached and worked with digital teams in some of the UK's leading brands.

in www.linkedin.com/in/trentonmoss

https://twitter.com/trentonmoss100